∾

"If you've ever felt like the path of faith you're on is a grand setup for a huge letdown, this is the book for you. One day you wake up, and the old patterns of belief and habits of thought fit the person you've become like clothes you've outgrown. You long for a new way of being, a new mode of inhabiting your faith, a new map to find this God, who looks and feels and sounds and acts so very unlike the old fire-breathing, finger wagging God of your evangelical days. The questions pile up and you wonder, 'what comes next? Is any of this worth saving? How do I build a new framework for my faith?' If any of you have ever asked these questions, as I have, so many times, if you have ever felt unmoored and unsure of everything except that you can't go back to the way things were before, consider this book fresh manna in the wilderness.

As I turned every page, I wondered how Jennifer knew my story, my struggles, my secret longings. Over and over again, I thought, 'Wow, I've been waiting on this book. I need this book.' I voraciously consumed every story and insight and challenge and question and invitation to go deeper. This book feels like someone turned on a flashlight in a dark room, making it possible for my groping, grasping, unapologetically feminist self to see a bit more clearly, to move a little more surely into a new and better way. Through Jennifer's hilarious stories, we encounter God in these pages, in the most unexpected ways. As Jennifer finds her voice, she helps us to find ours. And we are reminded that God is big enough for our questions, but that this same God might show up and offer us some rather unconventional answers."

—Brittney Cooper, Assistant Professor of Women's and Gender Studies and Africana Studies at Rutgers University, Cofounder of Crunk Feminist Collective, and Contributing Writer to *Salon*

"This courageous book—memoir, exploration, exhortation, inspiration for women, and more—is an audacious challenge to people of faith, especially Christians. But Jennifer Danielle Crumpton challenges me, a secular feminist, too, because this evangelical Alabaman refreshingly shatters every stereotype she meets. And she knows her stuff—early Gnosticism, black liberation theology, Indian mysticism, Title IX, Rumi's verse, Elizabeth Cady Stanton plus contemporary feminist vision—her intelligence and scholarship are insatiable. Yet she conveys both with warmth, not pedantry. This book is a brave, unique act of love by a brave, unique woman."

—Robin Morgan

"With wisdom, compassion, and inspiring conviction, Jennifer Danielle Crumpton encourages those raised in Christian traditions that mistake self-abnegation for faith—and feminism for sin—to separate manmade doctrines from the truth of the Gospel. This book does the very important work of reminding us that perfect love casts out fear."

—Carlene Bauer, Author of *Not That Kind of Girl* and *Frances and Bernard*

"With irrepressible wit and winsome irreverence, Jennifer Crumpton eloquently and persuasively achieves the near-impossible: she tears away the patriarchal veil that Christianity has traditionally placed over women's lives and finds astoundingly good news—not only for assertive and successful women, but for enlightened men as well. Blending incisive analysis of what's present in the Bible with refreshing reliance on what's absent (the wisdom of Sophia!), Crumpton becomes a trustworthy muse for a new way of being faithful."

—Galen Guengerich, Author of *God Revised: How Religion Must Evolve in a Scientific Age*

"With style, humor, guts, courage and grace, Jennifer Crumpton does what we've all been believing and praying is possible: she reaches deep into evangelical Christianity and finds a feminist spark powerful enough to reinvent the whole blessed tradition. She knows how strong the pull of faith, the pinch of gender conservatism, and what it costs to seek our own answers. My copy of *Femmevangelical* is underlined, dog-eared, and tear-stained. If you're a woman of faith who knows how to laugh, love, and fight, you must pick up this book."

—Joanna Brooks, Author of *The Book of Mormon Girl*

"With warmth, humor, candor, and intelligence, Jennifer Crumpton helps women take the lead in their faith traditions, traditions that continue to hold great influence in America and around the world. She boldly pulls back the curtain on male-dominated religious history, showing us how to challenge hierarchical 'power-over' and claim collective 'power-to' through authentically female spiritual practice and participation. *Femmevangelical* is deeply personal, reflective, and thoughtful, but also a powerful call to action for feminists of faith who want to express their spirituality by changing the world for women and girls—and for everyone."

—Gloria Feldt, Cofounder and President of Take the Lead, Author of *No Excuses: 9 Ways Women Can Change How We Think about Power*

"Jennifer Crumpton's *Femmevangelical* is an uncompromising declaration on behalf of women's dignity, and a heartfelt and bracing demand for justice, equality, and security for the lives of women and girls all around the world. The book offers a strong take-down of patriarchal versions of religion, notably Christianity (including the version of evangelical Christianity with which she grew up), and works with alternative sources, notably a variety of women's voices from a variety of social locations, to offer an alternative rendering of a woman-empowering, woman-affirming faith. Crumpton's version of Christian faith retains loyalty to Jesus but little loyalty to established forms of Christian orthodoxy. There is not much else that is 'evangelical' that survives here to join with the 'femme' of the title, but that says more about evangelicalism's continued failure to leave patriarchy behind than anything else. It has been entirely discredited for the author, so she looks elsewhere. A bracing, important book."

—David P. Gushee, Distinguished University Professor of Christian Ethics & Director of the Center for Theology and Public Life at Mercer University, Author of *Changing Our Mind*

"Smart, funny, and emotionally relatable, Crumpton is part of a new wave of feminine voices who are reinvigorating Evangelical Christianity in the 21st century. *Femmevangelical* is a wonderful and insightful book."

—Reza Aslan, Author of *Zealot: The Life and Times of Jesus of Nazareth* and *No god but God: The Origins, Evolution, and Future of Islam*

Femmevangelical

The Modern Girl's Guide
to the Good News

Jennifer D. Crumpton

CHALICE
PRESS

ST. LOUIS, MISSOURI

Scripture quotations marked (NIV) are taken from the HOLY BIBLE, NEW INTERNATIONAL VERSION®. NIV®. Copyright © 1973, 1978, 1984 by International Bible Society. Used by permission of Zondervan Publishing House. All rights reserved.

Bible quotations marked NRSV are from the *New Revised Standard Version Bible*, copyright 1989, Division of Christian Education of the National Council of the Churches of Christ in the United States of America. Used by permission. All rights reserved.

Scripture quotations marked (NLT) are taken from the *Holy Bible*, New Living Translation, copyright © 1996. Used by permission of Tyndale House Publishers, Inc., Wheaton, Illinois 60189, U.S.A. All rights reserved."

Scripture marked NASB is taken from the *NEW AMERICAN STANDARD BIBLE* ®, © Copyright The Lockman Foundation 1960, 1962, 1963, 1968, 1971, 1972, 1973, 1975, 1977, 1995. Used by permission.

Some of the material in this book appeared first in a different form at patheos.com and huffingtonpost.com.

Cover art: Martin Bentsen, MJB Films
Cover design: Jesse Turri

www.ChalicePress.com

Print: 9780827211025   EPDF: 9780827211049   EPUB: 9780827211032

Library of Congress Cataloging-in-Publication Data

Crumpton, Jennifer D.
  Femmevangelical : the modern girl's guide to the good news / Jennifer D. Crumpton.
— First [edition].
      pages cm
  ISBN 978-0-8272-1102-5 (pbk.)
  1. Women in Christianity. 2. Feminist theology. 3. Feminism—Religious aspects—Christianity. I. Title.

BV639.W7C78 2015
248.8'43—dc23

                                                          2014043424

"The moment we begin to fear the opinions of others
and hesitate to tell the truth that is in us,
and from motives of policy are silent when we should speak,
the divine floods of light and life no longer flow into our souls."

— ELIZABETH CADY STANTON

CONTENTS

PREFACE

In the early spring of 2011, I was sitting on the stiff, green-carpeted floor of the Christian Inspiration section of Barnes & Noble at 82nd and Broadway in New York City, surveying the spines of women's devotional books. I pulled them out, scanned their summaries, then pushed them back into their slots. It wasn't that they weren't full of poignant thoughts by great authors. It was that none of the narratives spoke to me where I was: somewhere between recovering evangelical and raging heretic.

During my last semester of seminary, I had surprised myself by unscrewing all the "twinkling marquee bulbs" from popular, traditional theology. Darkened glass shells of religion now lay shattered around my feet; I had not yet figured how to step out without getting cut. But I knew my faith could no longer support the same old story lines.

I was raised a conservative fundamentalist evangelical, but my life experiences had brought me to deeper resonance with progressive feminist theology, and I found myself stretched across the chasm between contradicting worlds. I had just broken off an engagement to someone who lived in another state, so my worldly possessions and plans for the future were scattered. Though I had known for some time that I had to make these changes, I was suddenly surrounded by the vast unknown. I was finishing grad school, nixing my plans to change cities, hunting for a new apartment in Manhattan, brainstorming job opportunities in a new career field, and beginning to date again with a whole new worldview to consider. At thirty-seven, I was a new person starting over with a new life.

Sitting on the bookstore floor, feeling overwhelmed, I was right where I was supposed to be. But I needed encouragement and solace, and found neither in the old religious tales and terms I used to use. In order to envision my future, I needed to reflect on my religious past and the numbing choices I had made out of fear and limitation. I needed a way to meet God and strengthen my spirit with new perspective, language, and rituals. It could not be the same tired "Christian lady" stuff about purity, piety, patience, prudence, and obedience. I needed a version of Christian faith that would empower me as a woman: one that would allow me to be subject instead of object, actor instead of reactor. I needed words and images to help me claim the wide-open potential of my new start with authority and power.

I wasn't a Martha or a Mary, a Ruth or an Esther, and had no desire to be put in their positions. I was more like an Abraham with a ponytail and an accidental angel tattoo, braving an epic, history-changing journey. I was a twenty-first–century Jacob with a woman's hips, wrestling shadowy images of the fully realized woman I could become, resisting invisible powers hell-bent on dislocating my joints. I had no interest in performing the role of good Christian girl. I wanted to be an effective woman: a productive, creative, consequential human being. I was no longer satisfied to be a dutiful lady-in-waiting; I was an aspiring leader ready to be seriously mentored in how to take on the world. I bet that's who you are, too. No Christian women's devotional I perused on that dark, blustery night recognized the implications of my metamorphosis and its effect on my faith. Academic works by brilliant female theologians developed and affirmed my feminist theology, but I could not sustain my spirit with scholarly jargon. I meandered home through a maze of grimy snow piles, empty-handed and feeling alone.

These pages are a conversation about this journey to authentic female faith. Since I had started to see both God and myself differently, how would I pray? How would I develop spiritually? Would I read the Bible? How would I build a new relationship with a different God whom I couldn't yet name or picture? Today, many women of faith are conflicted. We are moving away from the church and formalized Christianity in record numbers because of the gap between patriarchal doctrine and our real lives. Yet many want to keep the promise of love, hope, redemption, and resurrection that Jesus represents. At the same time, we long to adopt the feminine language, images and symbols that excite our imaginations: those to which we gravitate naturally and relate strongly, but which have been violently repressed within traditional Christianity.

Growing up in a Southern Baptist church, I recall posters encouraging tithing that featured quotes by Sue Monk Kidd. Her popular early Christian writings could support missions to "save souls." But recently, I happened upon her book *Dance of the Dissident Daughter: A Woman's Journey from Christian Tradition to the Sacred Feminine*. She chronicles her awakening to institutional Christianity's oppression and the need for feminism, and her calling to help women discover the divine feminine. She tells of her publicly criticized process of departing the church for life-giving, true-to-her-womanhood spirituality. I was floored to realize she wrote *Dance* in 1996, the year I graduated from college. Where had this been all my life? It reminded me that women must continuously tell our stories to combat the slyly suffocating, subordinating effects of male-dominant religion. Each story is important and cannot be repeated enough.

Every second, women around the world are suffering under the religious ideology that teaches and preaches that man is the head of woman, and woman was created for man. We have to constantly share experiences and experiments of rejecting the structure while reclaiming and strengthening our faith, because every day women are awakening. We need help keeping our eyes open and hearts filled.

I want to express deep gratitude to Brad Lyons, Gail Stobaugh, Rebecca Woods, Steve Knight, and the team at Chalice Press for believing in a book like this. To Karyn Carlo, for writing a life-changing note on my systematic theology paper. David Gushee, for giving me my first opportunities to use my voice and encouraging me to be honest about my experiences. My seminary advisor Christopher Morse, for composing notes that gave the gospel a whole new tune—one that greatly influenced this book—and for letting me curse freely in class in defense of Bonhoeffer. Thank you Hyung Chung Kyung for introducing me to a complex, vibrant world of death-defying goddesses. Hal Taussig, for discussing biblical scholarship and reminding me to be true to my interpretations of religious studies and my world. Rich Cizik, for sharing chats about faith and life. Galen Guengerich, for one amazing conversation that tied everything together. Donna Schaper and team for a transformational year in Judson's Community Minister program. Robin Morgan, for supporting my work across "secular" feminism and faith; your belief in me has made a tremendous difference. Thank you Monte Hillis for kicking fabulous heels with your pastoral robes, being passionate and smart about faith and justice, and showing me women "can absolutely do that." Alvin Jackson, for your strong spiritual leadership and inspiring words, and the congregation of Park Avenue Christian Church in New York City for being an open and encouraging place to grow. Thank you to so many friends and extended family for love and support. Deepest love and appreciation to my husband and partner David Ross, for fully believing in me and encouraging me to be exactly and unapologetically who I am. Thank you for showing me what real love is, and making me laugh every day. And a shout out to Jezebel, my furry and stalwart writing companion.

This book is for all the women who have searched for themselves in the Greater Story and had to take on an ill-fitting and even soul-killing role to be included. It is for anyone who seeks a devotional companion not written to prove a theological statement or uphold a religious institution, but to prove and uphold your individual experience, potential, and worth. Femmevangelical is meant to support the risk, hope, and faith it takes to follow your instincts and fulfill the real gospel: using our lives to create the world in which we were truly made to live.

INTRODUCTION

This Is the Good News

This is love: to fly toward a secret sky, to cause a hundred veils to fall each moment. First to let go of life. Finally, to take a step without feet. —RUMI

Thank God no one walked through the front door of my apartment building just then, because they would have stepped right into a big, messy puddle on the foyer floor. A shaking, sobbing puddle dripping mascara, with a red nose and one boot on, all dressed up from a Thanksgiving dinner and clutching a purse made of fluffy faux fur. That would be me. I had just gotten home, but I hadn't made it to my own door yet.

It all started about a half hour before, in one of those split seconds that move in slow motion because you do not quite know what to do. Your sense of the generally acceptable is telling you to stay put. But something takes over your trigger, fires your neurons with the strangely dangerous-yet-heroic fury of Bruce Willis wailing bullets at bad guys, and your muscles just shoot forward toward a bullseye you're not even sure you want to hit.

"The light will turn at any moment," the driver had prompted, and it was a very busy New York City street. The front door of the cab hovered open. I sat in the back seat weighing my options. *What is this guy trying to pull, inviting me to the front? Is it safe? Actually, I'm in his cab either way.* I considered jumping out and running for it. But then Bruce Willis gathered my bag, opened the back door, and made me do a little scurry up into the front seat. I pulled in my coattails and right suede boot and closed the door just as the light winked green and the traffic surged forward.

At the next stoplight, my right suede boot was on the floorboard and the cabbie was looking at the bottom of my foot like a skilled doctor checking carefully for a break. "Yes," he murmured, "you are an empathetic heart, but you've no need for much idle chatter or small talk. You would rather be alone thinking about the big picture than in fine company talking about nothing of consequence." He smiled as if recalling a good memory. "Ah, but in the right company you are boisterous and bawdy with your humor. You are weird even!"

His brow furrowed. "You are hesitant, but you will walk another path. As I was saying, you must first find your voice and not be afraid to use it.

You have a ways to go." I chuckled as I fumbled with my sock. What a trip. He went on: "You would make a good mother, but you don't gravitate to children. You could have five if you wanted. But more likely just one...or a half." His face blinked a reflection of green and he hit the accelerator again.

"Half a kid?" I snorted. He didn't respond. I was in my early thirties, but never thought about kids. I did not especially want kids, which was why my early marriage had broken up—the one I thought was the right next step during my mid-twenties in my hometown of Birmingham, Alabama, when a smart, nice, cute guy proposed after taking me to my favorite ballet. Looking back, it was an unspoken assumption that we would start a family and one day dunk however-many little heads at the Southern Baptist church down the street where I was baptized myself. That's what everyone did; I wasn't aware of any alternative. I had gone along with it until it hit me that what I really wanted was to raise the sheltered child still within me. Until the day back in Alabama in 2002 when my inner Bruce would no longer sit still in that skin, and made me hop out of the back seat of that life and into the front, steering a sharp left turn just in the nick of time.

By the time the foot-reading cabbie pulled up in front of my apartment building I was in tears. Actually, it had all started a little earlier that night, when, stuffed with a potluck Thanksgiving dinner celebrated in a small apartment packed with friends, I stepped out alone onto a tucked-away street in SoHo. The block was quiet for the city that never sleeps. My breath created ghosts for me to chase in the late night chill. I pulled my coat tighter, realizing I was going to have to walk four blocks to Houston Street, a thoroughfare, to hail a cab. I could see traffic whizzing by up in the distance and I quickened my pace, knowing there would be competition.

I had taken a few steps when I noticed a little yellow blip slow to a stop up on Houston. The rooftop hazard lights were blinking and the vacancy light was shining. *Damn, there's a cab freeing up way up there and there's no way I'm going to catch it.* New York City cabbies wait for no one. And in the shadows from a couple blocks away, there was no chance the driver could see me striding up the sidewalk, head lowered against the brisk breeze. But the glowing yellow rectangle didn't move, and oddly no passenger had gotten out. I finally approached the taxi and breathlessly peered in, expecting to see someone fiddling with a credit card or maybe throwing up vodka in the back seat, not unheard of on the late shift. But there was no one. I opened the back door and stuck my head in. "You open?"

"Well, hello!" boomed a rich, deep, joyful voice with an accent I couldn't place. "I've been waiting for you!" I smirked dismissively and slid in. "Seventeenth between 8th and 9th please." The driver turned his whole body around and looked at me through the plexiglass barrier. I was struck less by the odd gesture than his translucent, light grey eyes. Smiling brightly out of a peaceful face, he stuck a plump, well-groomed, golden-skinned hand through the opening of the barrier. "Good to see you; I'm Aman." I glanced at the official NYC taxi license always framed and bolted in the same spot behind the driver's head. Aman such-and-such, and his driver number. I hesitated skeptically. *You have already morphed into a grumpy New Yorker. It is Thanksgiving, after all, and you just had great conversation over a huge dinner while this nice man is out working hard all night.*

"Jenni," I smiled back, and shook his hand. It was warm and cushiony; as comfortable and dependable as the little red love seat in my living room where I curled up to read, pray, or write. I felt a bizarre sense of calm wash over me. He nodded, turned, and pulled away from the curb. After a more standard minute of silence, his eyes grinned at me in the rear-view mirror and he sang, "Jenni, there is something I have to tell you."

"Don't tell me," I whispered, and held my breath. Aman went on to deliver a cryptic speech I had become oddly familiar with over the preceding couple of months: *You have long let others make you feel uncertain, drown out your voice. But you are on an important journey. You must listen to yourself, not those who try to tell you who you could or should be. You will find out what you are meant to do, but you must come to believe you are able, worthy. People will try to silence you, but you must trust yourself. Speak up! Don't be afraid. You will have help. You have something to say that needs to be heard.*

I tried desperately to swallow the lump rising in my throat. My fundamentalist evangelical upbringing had taught me that people who claimed to be clairvoyant consorted with demons. Maybe they even were demons.

But I didn't really believe that "enemy" stuff anymore. I didn't buy that there were evil people roaming around with nothing better to do than trick Christians, trying to lure them off course with fanciful tales of the future, laughing maniacally while charming them to the edge of hell. But scare tactics drilled into your malleable child brain are hard to extract.

———

Aman talked unselfconsciously, like an excited child, all the way across town. I held my boot in my lap, studied his profile, tried to keep up, tried not to give in. I tried to act as if I found this hilarious, an amusing ride with a kooky cabbie, a great story about this unpredictable city that I now called home. But it was getting harder to pretend.

"Life is not what people think it is," he said. "Trust me, I have been on both sides and I know for sure." *Huh?* Did he mean drunk to sober? Dead to alive? Vice versa? He said something about living life counterintuitively, risking the status quo for real life, following the voice deep inside to find God...but I couldn't stop watching the city lights pass through his eyes.

Finally idling at the curb in front of my apartment building's stoop, I tried to get a good look at his face. His eyes were calm and knowing, the pale irises like those mysterious floating answers in the old Magic 8 Ball toys. The mood switched from jovial to serious. "There is more I should say to you," he said. "I will turn off my meter but we can keep the heat running and talk as long as you want, you won't have to pay. I'll answer all your questions." A cabbie not pushing people out the door, rushing for the next fare? Tears had begun streaming down my cheeks without my permission. I smiled and tried to act cool and collected, but I felt vulnerable and confused. "I really have to go," I croaked. I tried to hide my alarm at the fear creeping up on me in the suddenly claustrophobic cab: the fear of being duped into sitting to chat with a pleasant murderer, the greater fear that I had already been duped into hearing something that would butcher my carefully crafted worldview.

"Are you okay?" he asked, looking genuinely concerned. He suddenly seemed to be much further away and I felt bad about it, felt sad. I checked the meter for the total and pulled out my wallet. He gently held up his hand: "You don't owe me anything."

I ejected into the street with one high-heeled boot on and hobbled around the front of the cab. I hopped up the stairs, unlocked the front door of my building with jittery hands, and slammed it behind me. The foyer was empty. I tried to move toward my own apartment but couldn't. I stood with my back against the sunshine yellow wall and felt a storm moving in. *I have to pull it together. It's late and I have to go to work in a few hours.* I took a deep, steadying breath. *I'm going to go get in bed now,* I instructed myself. *The ad agency will be chaotic after the holiday.* I took a couple of steps across the patterned black and white marble. But then the floodgates opened and my feet failed me. I slid to the floor and the tears freely fell.

———

Actually, it had all started two months before, with two similar strange encounters. Those are stories for later. But what I realized in that particular moment was that my past had caught up with me, from 1,000 miles south of my foyer floor in Chelsea. I was crying with relief because someone had finally told me I was worthy enough to speak up, that what I thought and what I experienced mattered. I was crying with anxiety because something told me things would never be the same.

As skeptical and frightened as I was of what the cab driver had said, I believed him. What he had relayed to me in less than thirty minutes made more sense to me than the people or things I had believed for over thirty years. He had touched something intimate, and it wasn't just the bottom of my foot. He piqued my intuition, sparked my imagination, and connected with something deep within me that had never been invited out before. The longing for that feeling was something I had spent my life trying to tame, because the voice forced inside my skull since childhood said that such a longing couldn't be good. *I* couldn't be good. Aman had given me permission to be myself. He encouraged me to express, without fear or shame, what I knew to be true. He said the world actually *needed it.*

I was crying because I had been avoiding the fact that the great tectonic plates were shifting. The weighty foundation of the unmovable Christian tradition on which I rested, tethered in safekeeping my entire life, was starting to give with a deep groan. I felt threatened, as if about to be swallowed whole.

Most of all, I was crying because I was embarrassed at how little I really knew of my authentic self. As an introvert, I had always been overly self-aware. I was hypersensitive to subtle interpersonal dynamics, always worried about how I might affect people and situations around me. But as a young Southern Christian woman, I was so well-trained in the art of self-deprecation and so filled with self-doubt that the truth had to come from another mouth. Three others actually. Someone else had to describe a hidden part of me before I could accept that it might exist. Someone else had to tell me my story, give me another option for the next scene. A stranger had to make the veil fall, as Rumi, a thirteenth-century poet, philosopher, and scholar said.

Veils have for thousands of years been used to cover the heads and faces of women. Veils served to temper the lust of the men who looked upon us, whose excuse from the trouble of respect and self-restraint trumped our basic human need to be seen, trumped our right to see clearly through our own unobstructed eyes. Veils historically were to be lifted from the maiden only when she, as brokered bride, was fully transferred to the custody of her betrothed, her head. Veils were to make palatable a female presence in a house of worship, a symbol of modesty and subjection to her lord, who was not God, but her husband (1 Cor. 11:4–10). Rumi's veils likewise seem to be a metaphor for anything that holds us back from reaching the heights we were made for, whatever hides the flying triumph of who we really are, or obstructs our higher vision.

I cried like a scolded child when the first veil came down that night on my cold, dirty foyer floor. But, over time, I realized this had to happen, no matter how desperately my rigid religious upbringing tried to stop it. As I grew stronger and took more risks, more veils fell, each revealing a hint of a secret sky I couldn't see before. Now, each time another falls, I discover more space in my sightline, inviting me ahead. Many more must come down before I can truly be seen and known, and truly see and know the people and world around me. A cycle of scary risk, uncomfortable exposure, and new perspective brings revelation.

Together in this book, we will let a hundred more veils fall. We will aspire to let go of the life and faith defined for us. We will refuse the well-worn path, the ancient and narrow street, and take our first steps without feet. We may be strangers now, but to point one another upward and outward to the space waiting for us to fill it with flight is what it means to be women of faith.

Jesus promised that a new realm was in sight for those who would seek it, for those with eyes to see. He announced his mission by saying he had come to release the oppressed, to recover sight for the blind, to restore vision, set the prisoners free from captivity, and proclaim the jubilee (Lk. 4:18–19). To endlessly fell the veil is the work of God. It does not matter who or where we are right now, or what lies and false limits are holding us prisoner. The world needs us. We will have help. This is the good news. This is love.

DEVOTIONAL: Living Your Myth

> Conventional knowledge is death to our souls,
> and it is not really ours. It is laid on.
> Yet we keep saying we find "rest" in these "beliefs."
> We must become ignorant of what we have been taught
> and be instead bewildered.
> Forget safety. Live where you fear to live.
> Destroy your reputation. Be notorious.
> I have tried prudent planning long enough.
> From now on, I'll live mad.

This is an excerpt of a translation of the poetry of Jalāl ad-Dīn Muhammad Rūmī. Popularly known as Rumi, he was a Sufi mystic born in

1207 in Persia, now northern Afghanistan. A great scholar of the Qur'an, for centuries his words have transcended cultural and religious boundaries to illuminate the mysteries of God and the human condition. It is said that when he died in 1273, his funeral was attended by Muslims, Jews, Persians, Christians, and Greeks alike.

How would it look to "forget safety" and "live mad" (unconventionally) in the next steps of your career, relationships, and spiritual life? Where has convention, Christian or otherwise, served you less than well? Rumi said, "Do not be satisfied with the stories that come before you. Unfold your own myth." What does this mean to you? A myth is a legendary, epic, or improbable event that centers around a hero or heroine. It often begets a ritual or rite that people continue to practice into the future as a tribute to the central character's life or learnings. Which myths among the beliefs or legendary stories of your faith tradition encourage you, and which discourage you? When, where, and from whom did you first hear them? How have they manifested in your life?

What obstacles, triumphs, moral takeaways, and rituals might your own personal mythology entail? Imagine how you could make your life look more like the legend you would like to create for yourself and leave behind to guide other women. What spiritual tools, beliefs, or practices would help you do this, and what would hinder you? You are the heroine of your story; own it unapologetically. Do just one heroic act each day—say the hard thing, challenge someone's stereotype, tell your truth—to cultivate your sense of destiny. What you think and what you do matter tremendously to the world.

CHAPTER 1

Finding Your Femmevangelical

The most courageous act is still to think for yourself. Aloud.—Coco Chanel

The truth will set you free, but first it will piss you off.—Gloria Steinem

I will never forget the day a spritely seven-year-old girl in a Sunday school class I taught told me she wanted to be a concubine when she grew up. Her reasoning: God's favorite men received concubines as rewards, and if God gave a girl as a reward, that girl must be special. She had clearly picked up the term by hearing scripture read aloud, because she pronounced it correctly. I debated what to do, and decided I could not let it go. I relayed in G-rated terms that concubines were subservient mistresses collected by wealthy men as property, whether the women were cool with it or not, and it was wrong and corrupt. I figured she learned this in a "morality tale" about a famous leader God "blessed" with land, slaves, and concubines; so, clearly she was deceived by the set up. I certainly wished someone had helped me wise up earlier. So we talked about all God made her capable of and wanted her to be, even if she didn't hear stories about that at church.

I was struck that day by the consequence of allowing our religious stories—already seen through the male lens and written by the male pen—to continue being presented in the male voice without acknowledgment or interrogation. Had no one wondered what her takeaway might be? I understood her confused meaning-making; I was raised under the assumption that scriptural and doctrinal interpretations were formed and taught in a male-dominant framework because that was the framework of absolute truth. It would not have occurred to me that it could or should be otherwise. Sermons and Bible studies did not consider what it would mean to be a young girl hearing those glorified tales, or what they taught boys and girls about gender.

Religious values are still articulated in language, imagery, and literary styles that do not translate today. Yet this is the storyline within which girls are expected to learn God's character and come to trust God. This creates deep doubt and guilt-ridden uncertainty, not to mention backward ideas of who we are and what our purpose is. Even if we get positive messages about ourselves elsewhere, something about the intrinsic relationship of "God's story" to ancient negative portrayals of females is impossible to shake. Perhaps it is the underlying obvious: that in that story God never directly, definitively says or does anything about the horrific misogyny. And, unfortunately, Bible stories are used as literal morality tales, rather than as historical literature that could be used to teach girls to know when injustice and abuse are being perpetrated against us. Instead, the Bible is still widely used to perpetuate injustice and abuse.

The dangerous clinging to a rigid, nonsensical framework is one of many reasons why I am not the only one who has felt the shifting of the tectonic plates. A 2012 Pew Research poll heralded the rise of the "nones": the number of Americans who are religiously unaffiliated rose by 5 percent in the past five years, to an unprecedented 20 percent. Nearly one-in-three in the Millennial generation has no religious affiliation.[1] The Barna Group noted that among those 18–29 with Christian backgrounds, 59 percent have dropped out of church attendance after having once gone regularly, and half have been "significantly frustrated by their faith."[2]

In the 2011 State of the Church series, the Barna Group discovered that of the 60 American population segments they examined, none had gone through more changes in the past two decades than Christian women. Barna shows that Christian female church attendance sank by 11 percentage points to 44 percent, meaning a majority no longer attend church services during a typical week. We have also pulled the plug on our free labor as the volunteer backbone of the church, creating a 31 percent reduction in the "non-paid female work force at churches," Barna says. Bible reading plummeted by 10 percentage points; just four out of ten of us read the Bible in a given week, perhaps because our perception that it is the ultimate authority, or even helpful to us, has changed. The percentage of Christian women who believe the Bible is accurate "in the principles it teaches" has dropped 7 percentage points to 42 percent.[3]

Christian women who hold to the definition of God as the "all knowing, all powerful, and perfect Creator of the universe who still rules the world today" have declined, dropping from 80 percent to 70 percent. When I think of the misogyny propagated using that definition of God and God's words, the decline—or the refusal of that version of God—does not surprise me. And, if Barna's survey was only of Generation X and Millennial women instead of all age ranges, the drops would be even more dramatic. Yet, despite the increasing rejection of Christian dogma, Barna reveals that two-thirds of the women surveyed *still say their faith is important to them.*

What It Feels Like for a Girl

The divorce of spirituality and faith from institutional religion is not shocking. Rosemary Radford Reuther said it more than a decade ago in *Sexism and God-Talk: Toward a Feminist Theology*: "Religious traditions fall into crisis when the received interpretations of the redemptive paradigms contradict experience in significant ways."[4] In other words, the justice, blessing, and deliverance we are promised by traditional religion is not actually happening. We move on because the church's formula of religious revelation (who we are, what we should believe, and how we should behave) does not address our real daily lives and needs, and its kind of redemption does not make us feel redeemed. It makes us feel everything but.

However, despite keeping distance from institutional Christianity, the data tells us that it is too much for many women to depart from the personal concept of being Christian. We are reluctant to relinquish a connection to Jesus and the vision of a better world. There is still something valuable and desirable in that relationship (if we can make it our own) that haunts us with possibility.

Even as we press forward bravely and often stoically in the modern world, women do not want to lose our faith. We can't afford to lose hope. We know deep down that following the way of Jesus could and should be different from what we're taught by the church fathers. We imagine our faith can be lived without shaming or rejecting parts of ourselves. It can give us new life. But we must break down and move past the Christianity that has damaged our self-perceptions for so long.

Carlene Bauer is the author of *Not That Kind of Girl*, a coming-of-age memoir set against her struggles with an apocalypse-obsessed evangelical upbringing. She minces no words about the painful paralysis of self-doubt and fear brought on by fundamental elements of the Christian tradition, described by Bauer as a "hovering between a hunger for the world and a suspicion of it."[5] She recently wrote an *Elle* essay about her interview with ninety-five-year-old English author Diana Athill. Athill's memoirs helped Bauer sort through her own uncertainty, as she approached forty, about whether a life with a fulfilling career but no children was the one she had really meant to create for herself. Her relationship to confident intention was elusive. As Athill reflects on her life—her missteps and successes, her sometimes unconventional decisions and actions—Bauer is appreciative of Athill's unapologetic directness.

Bauer confides: "Having been raised evangelical, in a religious culture that requires looking to a book for answers, I've never been able to quit reading for revelation, for instruction, for affirmation."[6] Her fascination with Athill seems to stem from the sheer novelty of the type of woman who said, did, and pursued what she wanted without guilt, hesitation, or second-guessing. Bauer discovered that this type of woman could be respected, accomplished, and pleased with her life, instead of being condemned, dismissed, ambivalent, or regretful.

In the essay Bauer fights for her; even though Athill does not require it, Bauer seems to need to do it. Raised in a similar vein, I understand Bauer's urge to legitimize and reinforce Athill's way of being. It desperately has to be defended against institutions that would still seek to question a woman's autonomy and authority over her own life, and against those who would question Athill's morals because she said what she thought and did what she needed to do. "I think I was searching for a writer who would speak to me woman-to-woman," Bauer says. "Because I spent much of my young adulthood trying to figure out what God wanted for me rather than what I [wanted], I came of age—sexually, professionally, and otherwise—rather late, and it took the last half of my thirties to finish the job... My struggle to reconcile who I'd become with who I wanted to be took the form of debilitating bouts of self-doubt and sadness."[7]

I can relate, as can many women I know. I was raised to believe that God had a specific plan for me. I was to have faith that while I could not know what that plan was, it would only come to pass if I believed and behaved in certain ways. This makes it tough to make decisions about your life—much less to own who you truly are, who you want to become, what you want to accomplish, and what steps you must take to make it happen. Often, being a young Christian woman is to pre-define yourself on pre-determined terms that were pre-decided by someone who isn't you.

At a certain age, it was mysteriously exciting to be "faithful" this way, with the anticipation of opening a gift you cannot see or touch. But it had serious consequences. I spent a long time waiting for cosmic angels who knew my sealed fate to appear and point the way, and in the meantime I ignored and thwarted everything God had actually put inside me. Once I took charge of my life—which took some drastic but necessary forms, such as a divorce and a big move—I was haunted by guilt and the fear that I was risking being lost forever. I worried that it was disobedient to think for myself and act on my own behalf; and God would stop helping me survive the cruel, unpredictable, godless world out of disgust at my faithlessness. Instead, the exact opposite happened: I thrived. Like Bauer, it took until my thirties. My sole regret is that I did not wake up and start living autonomously and authentically earlier in life.

Following archaic rules, believing voices of authority that do not represent us, and waiting quietly for something to happen: those things are not faith. Everything you need to faithfully flourish is inside of you and up to you. Every positive, healthy, hopeful, loving thing you intrinsically know about who you are, your capabilities, and your potential impact on the world is God's voice. Even if it sounds still and small. It is your voice too.

The Revelation of Reality

We crave a spiritual home that we are also compelled to avoid, because traditional religion teaches that our faithful use of female power involves giving it up to God, also known as giving it over to the preference and authority of men, or men by way of female gatekeepers (often women with authority over us who raise us or teach us) who have been trained to uphold male dominance. Many of us find ourselves roaming our own modern deserts in search of an alternative that empowers us, lifts up our voices, and encourages thoughtful trust in our real, unique female experience. Perhaps you have lost friends or family support because you have questioned religion. You may feel a void if you stray from formal religion, since severing ties with even an unhealthy relationship is hard. But, unlike other difficult break-ups, traditional religion has probably been there since your earliest memories, and it really did promise you heaven.

Maybe you sometimes look back wistfully, remembering the simpler times when you were able to just believe and follow, and wondering what happens to your faith now. Or perhaps you've completely closed the door on the church and are not so sure God will open a window anymore. Does God still adhere to those cliches when one is technically turning her back on "his bride"? Maybe you're sick of all those gratuitous sayings and disconcerting metaphors anyway. After all, a historical bride of the biblical era was exchanged as property, with no say in her own life.

You may no longer know how to imagine, talk to, or experience the presence of the God you hope is there beyond rigid theism and doctrine. If you don't believe in the God that influential men have described for centuries with authority and certainty, is there a God to believe in? You are not alone. You are not wrong. It is our long-denied birthright to engage a system of belief that makes sense logically, experientially, and in its attitude toward our gender. We should not be asked to overlook elements of our faith that shame and belittle us. We should feel confident, worthy, equal, heard, holy. *Just as we are.*

Which is why we are here. There is a reality of the good news of Jesus that anyone can follow. It will require us to shed light on some of our darkest experiences with traditional Christianity, and the foundations of Abrahamic religious institutions in general. We must acknowledge where God is not present, so we can focus on where God really is. We have to unravel where our traditional beliefs came from, so we can begin to weave something different. This will involve a reframing of the big three: the Bible, church doctrine, and male hierarchy. Understanding what goes unsaid and untaught about our traditions can free us for deeper spiritual development. We will explore how we can envision, approach, and relate to the God who is free of damning ideologies and old gender-negative baggage. We will also devote time to meditations from other traditions and popular culture to help us color outside the lines. We are here to consider and create the future of something women say is still important to us: our faith. We are here to think for ourselves. Aloud.

Fighting Like a Femme

Femmevangelical started as an ironic nickname for my own faith journey. It melds the seemingly incompatible concepts of feminism and evangelicalism—albeit under a different definition of "evangelical" than what probably popped into your head just now. It is a description for following the way of Jesus as an independent, professional, modern woman. It is the convergence of critical thinking with the liberating gospel of Jesus, which will be clarified shortly. It is a term for being faithful to feminism, believing deeply in equality for women, and zealously working to convert the world.

Femmevangelical became a tool for starting conversations about how young women experience religious texts, liturgies, and teachings; and a forum to discuss why women are rejecting these traditions. It also became a platform for raising concerns about dangerous ways religious ideologies (including, but not limited to, sexism and misogyny) are still deeply entrenched in every facet of American life: politics, economics, social policy, education, literature, art, media, business, and popular culture.

What do I mean? Unequal pay and the inability to pass the Equal Rights Amendment in this day and age. The dearth of women at the highest levels of business leadership in America or representing us in government. The all-male Congressional panels pushing to legislate their opinions about what contraception women should use. Profits made by exploiting female bodies. The barriers to studying science and technology, and the documented sexual harassment that occurs when women do make it into those fields.

You have your own examples. My Roman Catholic friend Meagan wanted to be an altar boy growing up in the 1980s. Of course, she had it explained to her that little girls could not; only boys were allowed by God to have that sacred responsibility and prestigious position. It subtly affects what she believes she is worthy of still today.

In 2013, young women in several public high schools were told to "shut up" if they want God to approve of them and guys to date them. Richardson High School in Dallas, Texas hired a well-known Christian speaker named Justin Lookadoo to give his standard faith-based presentation to students at a school-wide assembly. Lookadoo, who speaks often at public schools nationwide, has created a website and two books (co-authored by Hayley DiMarco) to inform teens whether they are dateable or not. He calls it a "guide to the sexes" that promises teens that "in four weeks you'll be dateable!" Here is a sampling of what he told young women that God and guys expect. My translation of what girls will take away from it follows in italics:

Lookadoo: "Dateable girls know how to shut up. They don't monopolize the conversation." *God created females to be seen, not heard. Men could not care less what women have to say. It's all useless drivel and girls monopolize every conversation with all those pesky thoughts and feelings. Girls are so annoying and inconsequential that guys have the right to use the disrespectful phrase "shut up."*

Lookadoo: "You are soft, you are gentle, you are a woman. Don't try to be a guy. Guys like you because you are different from them. So let your girly-ness soar." *Guys will only want you if you are sweet and passive. So you probably shouldn't have a brain or boundaries, be competitive or assertive, or try to "wear the pants." If you are not the traditional vision of frilly femaleness (I hate the word "tomboy" because it focuses on "boyness" instead of the actual multidimensional girl) then you are a turn off. If you are actually strong, pretend you are weak. Never let on that you are smart or tough.*

Lookadoo: "Dateable girls aren't Miss Independent." *You are not a person of your own accord. You have no right to make your own decisions. And you certainly can't have a fulfilling life doing your own thing or being on your own. Besides not being autonomous, you should never prioritize yourself for any reason. Self-realization, autonomy, and personal fulfillment are not important for girls.*

Lookadoo: "God made guys as leaders. Dateable girls get that and let him do guy things, get a door, open a ketchup bottle. They relax and let guys be guys. Which means they don't ask him out!!!" *All guys are leaders who make all the best decisions and set up the structures of how things work. Females are not leaders; that's the way God planned it and wants it to stay. Males are the heads of females. Men are pursuers and aggressors; females are passive, accepting, and can only respond to guys who have first chosen them. Girls, stop trying to "do" things, choose things, or influence things. You're always messing up our ability to be guys.*

Lookadoo stresses that girls should rely on their "subtle beauty" and "the power of mystery" to get noticed. But here's the problem: if a girl spends her formative years concerned about creating an air of mystery for the sake of guys, her authentic self will also remain a mystery. Acting mysterious means she does not reveal or disclose herself, but actively obscures herself. If you look up "mysterious" in the dictionary, its definitions include "unintelligible" and "so enigmatic that one cannot interpret its significance."[8] A girl eventually becomes unknowable, unseeable, undetectable, and, in a sense, insignificant in the process of her withholding and hiding.

If a young woman's socio-religious environment threatens her with being "undateable" if she tries new things, talks through her thoughts and ideas, and unapologetically expresses her full personality, she will never learn who she is or how to speak her truth. She will not learn how to be honest with herself or forthcoming with others. She will lose confidence in herself.

Lookadoo's advice is a great way to get girls to remain confused and conflicted, infantile and underdeveloped, vulnerable, ashamed, and silent—all in the name of God. Though never stated outright in a school assembly, Lookadoo's ideas ring true as the silent code for girls when I was growing up in a predominately Christian community.

What if we instead teach girls to be fully, confidently, and unapologetically themselves? What if we made that the definition of being faithful to God? How about we teach girls that those people who are attracted to and respectful of their unique qualities are the ones with whom they should cultivate healthy relationships, while those who are disrespectful or hostile to a girl's authentic self are the ones she should reject and avoid? What if we taught girls that this is God's plan?

Women would thrive. Imagine how statistics of violence, abuse, and divorce might drop if the rules that girls accept from the get-go changed. What creates healthy, strong girls and women is being encouraged to freely, genuinely be everything God created us to be. Girls need to be told they are in charge of that process (not guys and their desires, sanctioned by Lookadoo's dude-god). It needs to be acknowledged that we are direct partners with God in our own growth and development—and in the relationships we choose. But in Lookado's type of traditional religious space, you must remain securely veiled (figuratively, if not literally) if you are a Christian girl who wants to date Christian guys, and be loved and approved by God. But wait, there's more!

Young men, as Lookadoo would have it, are to suppress their emotions and resist anything outside the "man code" that might resemble behavior appreciated or valued by the "opposite sex." Here are some rules for dateable guys (and my two cents in italics):

Lookadoo: "Dateable guys know they aren't as sensitive as girls and that's okay. They know they are stronger, more dangerous, and more adventurous and that's okay. Dateable guys are real men who aren't afraid to be guys." *Girls are emotional, messy, and weak; real men don't feel much but are way stronger. Guys are dangerous, which is a reminder to you girls not to challenge them. Guys are more cool and unpredictable. Girls are fragile and boring.*

Lookadoo: "[Datable guys] keep women covered up." *Because men are, of course, women's keepers, and women are but dolls for them to dress and undress as they deem appropriate. Since this is a religious talk, we will keep them covered up; even though the little sluts will still try to tempt us into sin, because they know that's what we really like, and they are here to please us.*

Lookadoo: "Dateable guys aren't tamed. They don't live by the rules of the opposite sex."[9] *Rules are only for girls, not guys. Females must be subdued and are only rewarded for performing behavior that guys like and following our rules. But guys should never be held back by being required to behave in a way that makes women comfortable, happy, equal, or safe, because guys are dominant and can do whatever they want. Guys are frankly more important and their freedom is without boundaries, while girls must live within the boundaries of our male context and desires.*

Unlike the advice for girls, the advice for guys is still put in terms of male agency and control and what guys need and want. What makes guys datable has nothing to do with behaving in ways that please female sensibilities, much less elevate or give freedom to girls. Girls are expected to change themselves with facades, such as prescribed beauty and a sense of mystery. Guys, on the other hand, are exempt from rules—especially rules about what girls desire or how they want to be treated. Sadly, Lookadoo is by no means the only voice who preaches and condones this. In fact, these messages are implicit in our daily intake of media, advertising and entertainment.

Most of us can recall experiences of the painful manifestation of those beliefs. We've experienced men—fathers, friends, teachers, relatives, or significant others—with no awareness that we have equal needs and are equally worthy to have them met. It makes us feel, and then eventually behave, as less-than and inconsequential. If we look back closely, many human tendencies, both male and female, have originated in religious assumptions that shaped society. This affects female psychological and spiritual development, which limits our educational experiences, career choices, economic security, leadership opportunities, and quality of relationships. It normalizes oppression and inequality, physical and sexual abuse, and crimes against women.

Not every Christian community espouses such toxic beliefs as Lookadoo's. But we recognize them in the cultural milieu. Listening to Lookadoo, it is easy to detect the dotted line from traditional gendered Christian assumptions, to a political climate in which an employer's insurance will gladly cover erection-stimulating medication for men who want more excitement, but refuses birth control options for responsible, healthy women. When we refuse to be treated this way, we walk away from the framework.

The Foundation of Femmevangelical

I was raised in a Bible Belt town that fought to keep tradition in place, and argued that changing it—even for the better—was to be sinfully unfaithful to an unchanging God. Feminism was a dirty word. I was never formally taught the concept. Anytime it showed up in the news, I was given a treatise about the ungodliness of these sinful, disgruntled troublemakers who were upset over nothing. By the grace of God, I was reintroduced to feminism later in life. Femmevangelical begins with a foundational feminist worldview, meaning simply that women are of equal status, value, and ability, and are fully human, autonomous beings. By "fully human," I mean that our gender is not less-than in possession of intelligence, conscience, autonomy, awareness, competency, agency, ability, worth, or purpose. We also do, in fact, have souls. If that makes you laugh, know that there still exist substantial numbers of people who believe females are a different, lower breed. By the same token, we are not—as stated in the subtitle of *Playboy* magazine—"entertainment for men."

Some women have issues with the term "feminism" or the myriad ways feminism has been expressed over the decades. But the fact is that our foremothers were historically forced by the ills and abuses of male-dominated society to actively demand equal treatment. We can acknowledge that gaining access to the vote, education, careers, and leadership positions demanded a women's movement. I am grateful for the wide range of women who used their limited resources and unlimited imaginations to address each situation in which women were held back, humiliated, or relegated to invisibility. We are deeply indebted to those who achieved victories in the face of great adversity, even death threats; who risked so much to get us where we are today—able to take many freedoms for granted. More and more young women recognize that we still require a women's movement to keep from backsliding, and to close the still-wide gaps in equality.

It is crucial that women influence critical decisions about how our world operates, and religion still has a strong hold on that operation. In order to create a more just, peaceful, and abundant life for all people, we must continually address the way women are socialized, viewed, represented, and acted upon. This effort requires the collaboration of feminism, womanism (Black liberation social theory and movement), Mujerista theology (Latina liberation), Korean eco-feminism (Asian liberation and ecological movements co-mingling the health of women and nature), and other equally important intellectual and social movements by diverse groups of women. Without these, we would be living a very different life today.

That said, the "Femme" in Femmevangelical evokes a broad female-friendly faith, honoring the feminine in whatever form, race, culture, ethnicity, expression, or disposition it lives. But the "femme" is also representative of a reversal of the archetype of the "femme fatale"—the fatal woman, the deadly female. The femme fatale is the glamorized stereotype of woman as evil temptress and our gender's primary purpose as sexual. It is the presumption that the feminine is most notably embodied as a seductress of compromised morals who threatens the status of men. It is a surprisingly widespread belief that women by nature are generally base, animalistic, sensual, and manipulative creatures largely devoid of rational thought and driven by desire.

The femme fatale storyline is that beautiful, cunning women manipulate men—who are the gatekeepers to everything in life—to get what they want. The femme fatale leads men into dangerous situations and makes them miserable (or cleans them out, or gets them thrown in jail, or kills them) in the process. It is the ageless cultural casting of the leading lady who deviously wrangles for power and gets the upper hand in the only way possible: by exploiting her mysterious sexuality. The narrative has the femme fatale employing a physical allure so irresistible that a man will do anything she says. In turn, while he is distracted and aroused, she can take anything she wants. Seduction is her only way of gaining power over men, leading them to their demise. The story assumes she wants to flip the hierarchy of male domination to her advantage, but she can only play the same old ineffective power game by the same old rules that actually turn out to work against her every time.

The femme fatale dates back well before characters played by Sharon Stone and Rita Hayworth, beyond Scarlett O'Hara, Lady Macbeth, and even Delilah, to—you guessed it—Eve. The story of the first woman tempting the first man to sin and ruining his life forever has been immortalized in the cultural imagination with a naked, voluptuous, flowing-haired Eve. In art and drama, she lowers her eyes and curls her lips in a seductive gesture toward Adam while holding forth a ripe, red fruit; which, of course, represents all sorts of juicy innuendo.

The myth of Eve in the garden of Eden has been used to insinuate that women today (via the mother of humanity) are impetuous, irresponsible, disobedient, and untrustworthy. And, as such, unconnected to God and in need of male control. We find this idea throughout the Bible (for example, 1 Timothy 2:11–15) and it has characterized cultural stories ever since. Theological interpretations by patriarchal philosophers and church fathers have unfortunately immortalized this false image of women.

Kim Krizan, the Academy Award-nominated writer of the films *Before Sunrise* and *Before Sunset*, wrote a modern take on the thousands of previous tomes on the femme fatale. *Original Sins: Trade Secrets of the Femme Fatale* is a satirical riff on history's obsession with female embodiment and desire as dangerous, and the almost laughable seriousness with which a woman's sexuality is simultaneously revered and feared. The description of her book reads:

> How to do really bad things! What's a woman to wear when she kills her husband? Or plays her detective for a sap? And ultimately, what's the appropriate ensemble for facing a firing squad?
>
> Who is the femme fatale? Since time began, every culture has been obsessed about her; women have wished to be her, and men—the dumb clucks—have connived to control her. Drawing on examples from history to Hollywood, this tongue-in-cheek handbook presents a new appraisal of feminine power: revealing how any woman can lay claim to her fatale birthright and have a hell of a lot of fun doing it. "Original Sins" is a guide for the woman who'd rather track her prey than be tied to the tracks.[10]

Even as she pokes fun at the whole cultural affair, Krizan touches on an important element of the historical set up: that women have been forced to choose between being helplessly tied to the tracks, or devising a way to distract their captors, wiggle loose and take a swing. It's not surprising that women reacting within the masculine dog-eat-dog paradigm went straight for the most obvious weakness of men with bared teeth, among other body parts, in defense of themselves. But, ultimately, when we assess the centuries of demoralizing consequences—and the fact that we still live in a male-dominated world—the survival and glamorizing of the fatale persona is a testament to the fact that women are still easily stripped of any real, deep personal power. The result is still a simultaneously sexually exploited and socially demonized gender.

This is not about how women choose to dress or express ourselves with fashion. I love a good red lipstick and have never met a pair of fabulous stilettos I didn't like. But the associated fatale stereotypes of the female *psyche* and *character* are insidious, limiting, and downright dangerous. I'm reminded of this every time a woman runs for political office and is harassed with lewd jokes about her body; judgments about her sexual attractiveness; and criticisms about her makeup, clothes, and hair. Add contempt for her "bossy" or "bitchy" attempts to "control" people and events (the same behavior that, for men, is simply called *governing*). A woman cannot lead without it being assumed she is trying to seduce, trick, or cause some sort of death. Yet, ironically, if she is not found to be seductive by society's standards, she is shamed.

Because this image of the femme fatale is still deeply entrenched in our society, Femmevangelical seeks to overturn the image of Eve as femme fatale. We know that women are fully equipped with intelligence, strength, trustworthy decision-making abilities, and a higher conscience that is crucial for the advancement of humanity. Yet we have historically been socialized to downplay, hide, or even forfeit those qualities. On the other hand, we get attention (if fleeting and shallow) when we behave as the sexy femme fatale; and not so much if we do lofty, honorable things; consider which images of women go viral. Femmevangelical flips the source of power to our critical vision and achievements, our ability to change the world, and our propensity to succeed without requiring the take-down of a man, or the take-down of our pants. Femmevangelical takes this flipped "femme" and the basic feminist stance of full equality and mixes it with the heart of the good news of Jesus, which needs a little more explaining.

Jesus, Interrupted

"Evangelical." Religiously diverse and politically loaded as the term is today, at its core it connotes a foundational relationship to the "evangel." The term comes from the Greek *euangelion*, meaning "the good news," "a good story or message," or "a reward for bringing good news." It is often referred to in Christian doctrine as "the gospel." This was not originally a term related to "truth" or "fact"—as in the phrase "that's the gospel truth"—but the two different concepts got creatively conflated around the thirteenth century. The evangel of Jesus has been stretched and built upon to encompass all sorts of things, but his good message was his proclamation that he was on a mission from God, circa years 28–30 of the Common Era.

Jesus launched his movement in his hometown of Nazareth in Galilee: a small, poor, labor-class village in the craggy hills of Palestine. It is said in the fourth chapter of the gospel of Luke that he went to the local temple where everyone knew him and stood up to make an announcement, and proclaim his good message. He unrolled the scroll of the prophet Isaiah and carefully chose a few lines from the beginning of Chapter 61. "The spirit of the Lord is on me," he recited, "because I have been anointed to proclaim good news to the poor. The Lord has sent me to proclaim freedom for the prisoners and recovery of sight for the blind, to set the oppressed free, to proclaim the year of the Lord's favor." (Lk. 4:18–19, NIV). Then he rolled the scroll back up. That was his gospel. Everything he did afterward flowed from and supported this. He never wrote anything down himself; only much later, after his death, did other people recount their experiences, perceptions, and interpretations of what he did, in their "gospels according to..."

However, on that fateful day in the temple in Nazareth, Jesus told those largely uneducated and vulnerable people staring at him with mouths agape that they had just witnessed the fulfillment of that ancient text. He told them he was there to make it happen. The audience understood the Isaiah passage he read in the political context in which it was originally written, as well as the context of their time; so his speech would not have been inspirational. Rather, it was a threat to their survival, to which they were barely hanging on during the violent Roman occupation of their land. Jesus' plan would stir up serious trouble; and the Roman governor was not averse to torturing and crucifying troublemakers, letting crows pick them apart along the thoroughfare roads where everyone could see. Hence, his community members got nervous and drove him out of the temple. For God's sake, he had just declared his treachery!

Those select few sentences from Isaiah—the original context being the time their ancestors (the Israelites) returned from Babylonian exile, in the 500s B.C.E. (Before the Common Era)—were chosen by Jesus because they would resonate: centuries later, Israel was once again captive to a foreign government. They were in need of hope, and a plan to change things to the way they should be: an autonomous people able to freely determine and live out their destiny. And that was what Jesus aimed to do: free prisoners, recover sight for the blind, set the oppressed free, and proclaim the year of the Lord's favor. He was speaking to his people in mythical terms they would immediately recognize and understand, even if it amounted to treason punishable by death.

This "year of the Lord's favor" referred to the fifty-year (some say seven-year) cycle of Jubilee outlined in the Torah in Leviticus. It claimed that, as a directive of the Hebrew God (Yahweh), during the Jubilee year people could take back confiscated personal property, slaves could return home to their families, and debts would be wiped away. In this context, Jews would be able to begin again under their own governance, worship their own God, and live their own way. For Jesus to say he was instituting the year of the Lord's favor out loud in a crowd in the face of Roman authority was not an ethereal spiritual thing. It was a bold political statement against rulers who were trampling the security, dignity, and culture of the Jews. It was a proposal to shift their current world of painful, negative experience into a new realm where the people were treated fairly and honored. Jesus said Yahweh noticed their dire circumstances and would not abandon them; he said there was a better reality they could hope for and fight for: the kingdom, or realm, of God.

The good news of Jesus was not that he was launching the creation of Christianity; his intention and vision had nothing to do with what later morphed into a new religion. Instead, Jesus was organizing his people under a common frame of values in order to demand change, to bring about a new order in which the vulnerable were empowered and the downtrodden redeemed to a new life. The good news was that Jesus was starting a movement to be respected and restored as a people, and they could all join in. In fact, success depended upon everyone joining in.

Just like today, people had different opinions, positions, and loyalties to political theories. Jews consorting with Roman rule to benefit from the oppression of their own people—such as tax collectors and leaders of certain Jewish religious sects who wanted the favor of Rome—vehemently opposed Jesus. They had found ways to compromise within the system and were doing fine, so why invite trouble? So, Jesus' good news of a rebellious plan mainly appealed to the sick and suffering, the homeless and hungry, the desperate and struggling, the social outcasts and people accused of criminality. If Jesus could convince a few rich or influential people to support the movement, it was because they had enough empathy to feel solidarity with people who others ignored and dismissed. They were ones who would risk their own status to advance the cause, to create a better life for others, even if it meant sacrificing their own positions in society.

Followers of Jesus had to be willing to risk their livelihoods, relationships with families and friends too intimated by Roman force to join, and possibly their lives. They would be opposed, mocked, and harassed. But it was the only way for things to change. It was the brave thing, the right thing, the divine thing to do.

The gospel of Jesus was the good news that even the most powerless people can come together and change things for the better, that we are meant to work alongside God to bring a new reality: the jubilee for all people. This is still the gospel today. Jesus never changed it; other interested parties across the span of centuries did. The real gospel of Jesus is difficult and messy, but, if we follow it, we can create a new world for girls and women today. We can uphold society as God meant for it to be: a place of dignity and freedom, where all people are equal and take their rightful place. To be evangelical, then, is to believe this message, and to bravely act upon it.

To be Femmevangelical is to know this good news is true for women of all ethnicities, races, and religions around the globe; and to act with intention and vision to establish a new culture that is respectful, safe, and full of unrestricted opportunity to live into our leadership and purpose, no matter what form that takes. The gospel of Mark tells us that "...Jesus went into Galilee, proclaiming the good news of God. 'The time has come,' he said. 'The kingdom of God has come near. Repent and believe the good news!'" (Mk. 1:14–15, NIV). Society was to repent from the old ways and act in accordance with the gospel, in expectation of a new realm coming to pass.

Much like "evangelical," the term "repent" also has a meaning often misunderstood. We perceive the need to repent as shameful, because the concept has been misused by religious leaders to belittle and corral people into a manageable order under a hierarchy of power. However, the Greek *metanoia* implies a shift in perception after a life-changing realization. It hints at a change of heart following a meaningful experience; the act of changing one's own mind to accept a new reality. It has nothing to do with guilt, finger pointing, punishment, confession, or suppression of certain aspects of ourselves. It means to turn away from or reject one thing, in order to buy into something different.

The act of repenting, or shifting one's consciousness into a new vision of the way things are or can be, is for the sake of the person herself. Repenting has to be done so that she can now exist in the realm of expanded possibilities for new ways of being. It is not to appease anger and wrath that God supposedly feels. It is not to satisfy religious authority or doctrinal mandates. A person decides to repent, or change her view of reality, so that she can take part in something better. Goodness knows Jesus never did or said anything for the purpose of getting into the good graces of the religious establishment—in fact, quite the contrary. Repenting is necessary in order to see the coming realm of God. It is a felling of the veil.

Jesus did not establish a new religion, especially not in the middle-class and wealthy suburban Americana context in which we understand and practice Christianity today. He did something much more universal and inclusive. He introduced the potential for a different reality and modeled "the way" to bring it about. A few famous leaders and world changers who have "gotten" the gospel have been following this way over the centuries, and the heroic risks and counter–status quo messages of people such as Nelson Mandela, Mother Teresa, Martin Luther King, Jr., and Mahatma Gandhi have moved humanity forward in profound ways.

This kind of change happens when people stop morality-slinging, hyper-defending their status quo, and relentlessly debating the meaning of every last word of that complex amalgamation of ancient stories called scripture—and really start following Jesus. Ironically, Jesus pointed this out in his day, too. If we follow suit, we can see each other as human beings and zero in on what needs to be done to turn the old, oppressive kingdom into a progressive, productive society. The notion that we can turn (repent) and accept (believe) a better way of being is gaining momentum—even in the face of rigid, angry opposition—as it sparks passion in the hearts of new generations. Equality is still not a real priority in many mainstream American religious traditions—at least not with the same emotional outcries and political vigor used to defend traditional beliefs. As Jesus said, not all have ears to hear and eyes to see; fertile ground is required for seeds to grow. But the real gospel continues to assert itself in contemporary forms over the course of human history, as we wake up and wise up. As theologian Theodore Parker and Martin Luther King, Jr. both proclaimed: the arc of the moral universe is long, but it bends toward justice.

We have witnessed that slow but certain movement in the United States, in critical moments like the passing of the 13th Amendment to the Constitution, abolishing slavery, and the 19th Amendment, which allowed women to vote. We saw it when the Supreme Court struck down Proposition 8, which banned same-gender marriage. These rare moments of hard-won change and triumph are proof that Jesus still walks among us. We still have far to go, and laws on the books, though necessary, do not immediately release hatred and fear from people's hearts. But those who perceive the heart of the gospel know that the good news—the reality Jesus put in motion—sets us on a trajectory toward justice, loves us into freedom, fights for us every moment.

Called to Follow, Created to Lead

Women of faith must put up a fight for our traditions in the way of Jesus. We cannot just walk away. Jesus proclaimed the gospel of freedom, equality and release from oppressive systems, but we have to do our part.

Jesus' people had been rallied by dissidents and messiahs before. But Jesus brought something different, universal, and transcendent to the scene: a fervor for justice that could apply to everyone for all time. This place of holy rebellion in each of us is where the coming realm of God hangs. People are made of passion; it's just a matter of pointing it in the right direction. Misdirected, it can cause great harm. Miseducated, it can promote confusion, oppression, and instability. Unstimulated, it folds in on itself and smothers us. Given a life-affirming purpose, it can propel us into a new reality.

After his crucifixion, the world would try to capture Jesus' unique leadership, notoriety, and charisma and harness it for various agendas, positive and negative. His gospel and his God's name have been invoked to sanction rape, violence, torture, enslavement, and the suppression of groups of people. His name is misused to give unlimited, unquestioned authority to religious elite who abuse power and people. His name is invoked to twist ancient scripture into modern discrimination. It's time for us to take his style and substance back.

My friend Donna Freitas is the author of many important books, including *Sex and the Soul: Juggling Sexuality, Spirituality, Romance, and Religion on America's College Campuses.*[11] I remember the first time I met her, after she stood up among hundreds of people at a conference and deftly challenged an assertion by a panel speaker. She looked like a goddess in a flowing light blue sundress, and her observations flew like darts smacking a bullseye in rapid succession. I immediately wanted to be like her.

When we met up in line for lunch that day, I was surprised to hear her identify as a staunch, lifelong Roman Catholic. She was hip and progressive and did not seem like someone who would be strict about tradition or agree with the dictates of the priestly office. She explained that while there was so much about the Catholic institution's rules and behaviors she disagreed with vehemently, she refused to bow out and disengage. If she and other progressive women left Catholicism, she explained, it would remain ensconced in patriarchy—"father-rule" or social structure marked by supremacy of men—restricting women and other "unholy" outsiders in many ways.

Those who challenge a system sometimes need to stay within it in order to change it, no matter how frustrating and futile it feels. Donna knows that to get that powerful behemoth to recognize and include the wisdom, leadership, and experience of women in the higher ranks of its global influence, she has to care enough and be strong enough to stick in it—like a burr in its fur. Her voice and participation matter deeply, because the Roman Catholic Church affects the beliefs, decisions, and futures of hundreds of millions of women around the world. It's not everyone's calling; but, if Donna left, she would be forsaking all the women who are looking for God there.

For women, desperately trying to understand our everyday experiences is at the heart of understanding who God is. It has to be, because so much of so many women's daily experience around the globe feels like hell: street harassment; rape; domestic violence; poverty; sex trafficking; genital cutting; the denial of education, economic opportunities, property rights, and authority over their own bodies—just to name a few. If half the population experiences a living hell, to various degrees, and Christian institutions deny the gravity of our experiences and abjure widely appointing us as leaders with solutions, then where do we turn? If our refuge refuses us, exerts oppressive control over us, and tries to call it salvation, then what is our recourse?

No matter what our spiritual persuasions—even those who have understandably left religion and the church out of frustration—it is crucial that we do not leave Jesus to the powers that be.

DEVOTIONAL: I Am

Do not be ignorant of me at any place or any time... For I am the first and the last.

I am she who is honored and she who is mocked / I am the whore and the holy woman

I am the wife and the virgin / I am the mother and the daughter

I am the limbs of my mother... I am a sterile woman and she who has many children

I am she whose wedding is extravagant / and I didn't have a husband...

I am the idea infinitely recalled / I am the voice with countless sounds...

I am both awareness and obliviousness / I am humiliation and
pride

I am without shame, I am ashamed...

Do not be arrogant to me when I am thrown to the ground...

Do not laugh at me in the lowest places

Do not throw me down among those slaughtered viciously...

In my weakness do not strip me bare / Do not be afraid of my
power...

I am she who exists in all fears and in trembling boldness

I am she who is timid... I am witless and I am wise...

Why do you curse me and revere me?

... I...of the heart...of the natures... control and the uncontrollable

I am the coming together and the falling apart

I am the enduring and the disintegration...

I am judgment and acquittal... I am she they call truth, and
violation

You honor me...and then you whisper against me...

I am what anyone can hear but no one can say...

I am what everyone can hear and no one can say...

This is a series of excerpts of scripture from *The Thunder: Perfect Mind*,
a text discovered in 1945 in the caves of Nag Hammadi, Egypt, along with
fifty-one other ancient documents. It was originally composed in the Coptic
language, indicating probable Egyptian origin, and it is thought to have
been written between the first century B.C.E. and the third century C.E.
(C.E.).[12] The author is unknown, and the feminine voice and experience it
relays may be one reason it was never mentioned in other ancient literature
and was left out of the New Testament canon.

Today, it is a religious text that shocks the senses in that it resonates
with women's lives. Not surprisingly, it has not been made available
in the mainstream for study, meditation, or inspiration. Nowhere in the
Bible does a feminine voice speak without the masculine words, thoughts,
and experiences of male players being put in her mouth. (Even Mary's
"Magnificat" is a political statement). We will talk more later about how
scripture was canonized with the ideas the church fathers thought were
relevant. But let's ask this question now: Why is it that canonized scripture
is considered right or real, and this one wrong and false? Why is the
Bible—written by mortal men who interpreted life from their gendered
perspective—sanctioned as the "word of God," while this, written in

similar structure by another human being interpreting God and life from the female perspective, is not? What does the male control of scripture from many centuries ago mean for religion and society today? For girls and women—now, and in the future?

Meditate upon the excerpts of *The Thunder: Perfect Mind* scripture before bed for at least one week. How do you feel when you fall asleep and wake up? What dreams arise? What would it be like to say those words to God as a prayer? Try it! What do the words mean in your own life? Jot down notes about what it evokes each time you read it. Does it articulate anything about your faith journey? Your relationship to the world around you? Your dreams, or the obstacles to your dreams? What words or images allow you to see yourself in this woman? What does her life of contradictions, of being simultaneously desired and rejected, signify? What does her combination of triumph and struggle, strength and vulnerability, mean to you? Write a few of your own lines that begin with "I am..."

Watch the Prada parfums short film *Thunder Perfect Mind* by Jordan Scott and Ridley Scott, which debuted in 2005 at the Berlin Film Festival: https://vimeo.com/12520881. Does using the scripture to thematize the surface complexities of a woman and the visible contradictions of her image in society bring it alive? Does using it commercially to promote an expensive brand change it for you? Does it diminish the text, heighten it, make it more real, or make it seem unattainable to link it with a high-end fashion house? What view does it reflect of women? What story do you come away with?

Watch the 1991 film *Daughters of the Dust* by Julie Dash, the first feature film by an African American woman distributed theatrically in the U.S., which opens with a long citation of *The Thunder: Perfect Mind* and uses its perspective to connect concepts throughout. (You can find it on Amazon. com.) How does this narrative bring to life the scripture for you? What new angles and possibilities do you see?

CHAPTER 2

A Modern Muse

Miracles are a retelling in small letters of the very same story which is written across the whole world in letters too large for some of us to see.

—C.S. Lewis

A bird doesn't sing because it has an answer, it sings because it has a song.

—Maya Angelou

Eva Shang was a seventeen-year-old freshman at Harvard University when she e-mailed me in the fall of 2013. An accomplished activist and the Harvard Campus Editor-at-Large for *The Huffington Post,* she is intelligent and mature beyond her years. She explained that she had been agnostic all her life; but in the months before she left home for college, her mother seemingly got nervous about the transition and made her attend a Presbyterian church every Sunday for several weeks. Eva was taken aback by what she witnessed and experienced in the church. Because her mind had been trained for asking critical questions about the world, she could not fathom some of the strange ideas the churchgoers believed without hesitation about God and humanity. In one of her notes, she wrote:

> It's been unsettling to me how certain and unquestioning everyone in the room is, when I have so many questions, especially from an equality standpoint... Why is it that a God who supposedly stands up for the oppressed would choose as his son a white male, just like every other person in power ever? Why is it that a Western religion would be The Right One that sends all the others to hell? Why is it that riches and glory (supposedly) mean nothing, but God still bestows them upon Solomon (and others), along with the 700 wives?[1]

What she noticed immediately upon her first exposure to church is that Christianity—the Bible, doctrine, and hierarchical structure—is full of contradictions, superstitions, and narrow assumptions. The church claims to stand for universally upright values; yet many abide and promote sexism, racism, homophobia, and the dismissal of other religions and cultures as obsolete or evil. Biblical characters get absurd rewards in the form of riches, power, and collections of women's bodies, regardless of bad behavior. Those who hold certain core beliefs—namely, that only traditional Christians who say the right formulaic salvation prayer are saved and going to heaven—seem to ignore the potential for divisiveness and discrimination, while simultaneously attempting to stake claim to universal truth.

The other thing Eva noticed was that Jesus is presented and spoken for as a white guy with middle-American, middle-class sensibilities—despite being a poor, oppressed, Middle-Eastern Jew. No one at her church ever mentioned that he was from Palestine and had almost no power in his own time and context; or that he in fact did not create a European and American religion. Christians in the Western half of the world (or those converted by Westerners in other parts of the world) use images and terms that make him into something other than what he was, so that he is "acceptable" for their American or European brand of savior status. In reality, he would have had dark skin and spoken Aramaic, a Semitic language related to Hebrew and Arabic. He was an activist working to resist and overcome the troubling reality of the occupying government and the Jewish religious figures who collaborated with Rome's oppression. Jesus never wrote anything himself that we have discovered, and, considering the socioeconomic status of his community of origin, scholars believe he was illiterate. (He would have known from a lifetime of temple gatherings and Torah study what the scroll of Isaiah said).

Hence, his story was written by other people—many who never met him—decades after he died. Ironically, the church built around the name of Jesus misses so much about him worth following: his unabashed boldness and bravery from a place of no power, his unorthodox challenging of authority, his grassroots organizing of a radical social movement against a massive Roman force, his affinity for those who struggled, and his willingness to risk everything to make things right for those who were overlooked and mistreated. Eva went on to observe how this becomes problematic:

> Another major issue I've been struggling with is the idea of say, Gandhi being deemed "not wise"; because in church small-group sessions, everyone went around and repeated that "True wisdom stems from God's word." ...And if Jesus is the Only Way to God, that means everyone else on earth is eternally damned, which makes very little sense.[2]

The cognitive dissonance that so many experience with Christianity is primarily caused by this: we have allowed ancient stories written by fallible men for the purpose of addressing their own ethnic and cultural questions from thousands of years ago to dictate what we are supposed to believe about God today. To top it off, we have suburbanized it. We have codified those stories and sayings—and their centuries-old interpretations, filtered through institutional power structures—into a presumed immortal truth befitting the status quo, legitimizing it in perpetuity as the final and fixed word of God. Then we tied one self-centered version of it to American patriotism and nationalism. We have created symbols, images, and metaphors that we worship. Anything God has shown us since, through the course of our growth and development as a diverse human race, has been marginalized or labeled heretical and illegitimate.

Eva's concerns mirror those held by many who were inculcated from childhood. If we think deeply, we eventually butt up against the same disconcerting issues. As I wondered what it would look like for feminist women who do not automatically buy in to religious assumptions to follow the way of Jesus, she became a modern muse for developing the characteristics needed to move away from ancient pedagogy into progressive action. Here are some important things feminists of faith must do:

Question Everything

I have gotten hundreds of questions from women who have learned the hard way not to raise contradictions and suspicions to the light in a traditional church setting. Many have been taught that it is blasphemous to question religious teachings. But the questions are brilliant, healthy, and necessary: Why would God plan for us to find peace and rest in a spiritual salvation achieved purposefully by a violent, sacrificial death? Is making us into forgiven Christians what Jesus' death was really for? From what do we actually need saving? How does love win after the crucifixion if we are still forced to play by the rules of the hierarchy and male power code that Jesus actively opposed during his life? Why is the Bible, which is about one group of people in one place and one time in history, extrapolated as God's story and rules for all of humanity? If God is really omniscient and omnipotent, and Jesus is the savior of all, why do we have all the same problems recorded in the Bible: war, occupation, oppression, famine, and sexual violence? Since not much has changed, was Jesus' life, death and "supernatural" visit to Earth in vain? And, if he is coming back to kick ass, why is he letting so many suffer in the meantime?

If the Bible is truly the literal word of God for all times, why is it full of language and stories used to stifle the freedom and authority of women? Why would the God of the universe say that women—half the human population—should be quiet and submissive under the headship of men, who are no better or more capable than we? Why would an all-knowing and all-powerful God encourage prophets and preachers to blame and punish women eternally for the supposed "fall of man"? As Benedictine nun Sister Joan Chittister lamented when given an award by Feminist.com at the 2013 Our Inner Lives event in New York City: "Almost every religious tradition says women were second to be made, first to sin."

This tradition explains a lot about our world today. And there are consequences: the acceptance of the rape culture as normal; the continuation of child marriage in many locations around the world; and the fact that, in 2014, the United States ranked 98th in the world for percentage of women in the national legislature, just to name just a few.[3] Why would an omnipotent God create or allow any of this? The truth is that God did not. We must question everything if we want to recover our faith. The point is not to try to disprove Christianity, although a lot about it warrants disproving and delegitimizing. The point is to get an understanding of what is not following Jesus, so that we can legitimately follow Jesus. And Jesus questioned everything about his society, including the motives of religious, political, and economic operations. He challenged traditions.

Call It Like You See It

Sometimes I look back over my life and wonder how many times I have known in my heart of hearts that something was not right; yet, out of duty or lack of confidence, I defended my religion. I was intimidated by authority and the harsh consequences of breaking the rules. Our gut feelings and perceptions about the impact of structures around us must be respected, called forth, and acted upon. The health and futures of girls coming behind us are at stake. We must be bold enough to call things like we see them.

For example, if you watched coverage of the latest papal conclave unfold in March 2013—marked by long processions of men in ornate robes playing out a ritual from centuries past—you witnessed the magnitude of the systemic male hold on not just souls, but also international policy. The pomp and circumstance of an event such as that evokes a certain sentimental beauty in its deep tradition, but sentimentality obscures the oppression that tradition has endorsed and enacted over history. Cloaked in secrecy, unchecked power and influence is still held today by a small group of elite men and their centralized resources. They operate outside the law, as we have seen in their handling of the endless child sexual abuse cases. Members of the institution do some wonderful work, but many also hold fast to dangerous ideas about the subordinate place of women in their hierarchy and women's rights to make decisions about childbearing. Hundreds of women in Ireland have recently revealed that, over the past several decades, their pelvises were sawed in two during childbirth without their knowledge by doctors who were following the orders of the church—which said this debilitating torture would allow women to have larger numbers of children.[4] What does your gut say about that?

The recently elected Pope Francis, while more thoughtful, social justice-oriented, and outspoken than most of his predecessors on issues such as poverty and inter-religious cooperation, stated unequivocally that the Roman Catholic Church will never change its doctrine on the place of women. Women are banned from certain formal leadership and ordination because the priesthood is based on an elevated spiritual character the Catholic Church believes only men possess. Church teachings also say Jesus only picked male apostles, which is simply not true; there were many women who traveled with Jesus and helped with his mission on many levels, despite the male-centric social mores of the time. Additionally, the church doctrine points to the fact that Jesus Christ was male, and when men participate in the priesthood, they act *in persona Christi Capitis*, or "in the person of Christ." Priests consider themselves the head of Christ's body, the church, authorized to act with Christ's authority in Christ's place.

Many speculated that the somewhat progressive inclinations of Pope Francis could lead to a change in this antiquated, dangerous thinking. But in response to a reporter's question about this hope, Pope Francis rebutted: "I don't know where this idea sprang from. Women in the church should be valued, not clericalised. Whoever thinks of women as cardinals suffers from a bit of clericalism."[5] In other words, lowly outsiders who see potential for such a change are overstepping their boundaries by even imagining, much less suggesting, the Vatican could or should see women differently.

Go back and let his exact statement sink in. Keep in mind that if women were allowed to become cardinals, not only would those women have influence among local and regional congregations—a direct connection to the development of human spirituality and religious understanding of the world—but they would also be part of the exclusive group that elects the Pope. Which would mean that, eventually, a woman might be named Pope. She would be the most powerful religious figure in the world—with her own city with its own zip code, with its own statehood and seat at the United Nations, with an estimated $9.23 billion in the privately held bank at the Vatican,[6] holding the ear of world leaders, and wielding the ability to influence the way the world works. Can you imagine the difference this would make for women and girls all over the world? However, the Roman Catholic Church finds this prospect to be the opposite of inspirational.

Let's listen more closely to the Pope's defense of the all-male gig in the global Catholic institution: *"Women should be valued, not clericalised."* This statement exposes the type of tricky language used to placate and dismiss women for centuries. To be valued as human beings should be intrinsic and assumed; it should be ridiculous to even state something so obvious. Here, the term "valued" is used to distract us from the issue at hand: that women are denied formal leadership and high-level influence in the single most-powerful religious institution in the world, because self-interested men claim to speak for God. And they claim God says women are not allowed to be in these positions.

The Pope's phrasing that women should be "valued, not clericalised" creates a sneaky dichotomy. The notion of women clerics is purposefully put opposite the idea of women being valued. We can be one, but not the other. The ideas are craftily positioned to be opposed: one is right so the other is wrong. This sentence structure would make sense if the Pope were saying, "Women should be valued, not dismissed," or, "Women should be valued, not repressed." You know, something the opposite of valued. The concept of women in power and the potential of women's leadership is the opposite of valued, is what he is saying. We are valued as long as we stay in our subordinate, controlled place. But if you are not listening closely, it sounds nice.

This manipulative sleight of hand with language is exactly what we find throughout centuries of Christian biblical interpretation, doctrinal rules, and hierarchical systems. It provides one gender with the false authority to tell the other half of the population that we can only be valued in the way they want to value us. It sets men up to decide and enforce what and how women can or cannot be, and to use "God's authority" to do so.

Ironically, on the local level, the Roman Catholic Church is an institution whose daily get-your-hands-dirty activities are primarily carried out by females. In 2013, the number of religious sisters in the U.S. was 51,247, while the religious brothers only numbered 4,407. Globally, sisters tally 721,935, while brothers add up to only 54,665.[7] The truth is, women are not allowed to be clerics because the institution, from the Pope down, irrationally believes women to be less-than men in the natural order and unequipped for executive leadership, for which this religion believes God made man exclusively. Yet women are out there doing a great deal of the hard work that keeps the institution running.

And, of course, this stronghold and abuse of power are not just within the Roman Catholic Church (the latter simply receives more worldwide news coverage). Men are the majority of "CEOs" of Protestant churches, and many of these communities still claim that only men can know the mind of God and communicate with God as one's intercessor. Sex crimes, domestic violence, and subordination are found here too. It is imperative that when we see, hear, or experience these things, we call it like we see it. No matter how many religious, political, and traditional sensibilities we offend, this is more important: letting little girls know that not everything they are taught by "authority" is right, permissible, or true in the eyes of God.

Talk about God in Your Own Terms

When those of us who question or walk away from formal religion leave, we tend to stop talking out loud about God. We do not have formal occasions to use religious language anymore, which can be a good thing considering most of it is male-centric and articulates a passive, superstitious worldview. But we also lose the opportunity to share our faith and beliefs with others, and frame them in words that empower and uplift women, drawing us closer to God.

Progressive Christian writer Tony Jones once observed that progressive religious leaders tend to steer clear of defining God by traditional methods, so as not to keep people of faith limited to the dark ages. (The term "progressive" is used here to classify forward-looking Christians who are willing to change old belief sets to support equality and improve people's lives through progress and new thinking.).[8] The problem, he said, is that meanwhile, traditional conservative Christianity imprints and enforces absolute statements about God's character on the majority of Christians (and non-Christians, for that matter). In infamous cases, the focus is on what God hates; but all around, the God-talk claims unquestioned knowledge of God's thoughts, judgments, and demands.

It was pointed out, as such, that progressive Christians effectively give God up—or give God over—to the rigid definitions and potential abuses of the old traditional Christianity. "Their [conservative Christian] people pretty much know what they think of God. It's well-known and on the record," Jones said.[9] That certainty attracts flocks of loyal members who feel comfortable with limited, cut-and-dried answers, no questions asked. In the meantime, progressives are missing out on the chance to talk differently and normalize a God who loves all people, resides in all people, created all people equally, and sends no one to hell.

A different kind of God-talk is needed to mine the good from the Christian tradition. We need to hear and know that God is love. We need to know God is greater than any given circumstance in which we find ourselves. It is also necessary to create a new dialogue about the God we know exists, but whose characteristics are not popular with the old guard. For instance, in order to ask society to treat women equally and with respect in the name of God, we need to be able to point to a God who is just and fair—not jealous, petulant, and retributive. We need to break God-talk out of the biblical era and start talking as if God is with us here and now, and even ahead of us, drawing us forward as we evolve in inclusiveness, empathy, and unity. Yet even many progressive churches still talk, sing, preach, and pray primarily in terms of a controlling, warring, vengeance-obsessed, and hyper-masculine Father God, because new language to take the place of the traditional jargon has not been fully developed or universally captured, recorded, and adopted. We have been socialized to accept centuries-old language as harmless—hey, we know "mankind" includes us all, and the Bible is old!—but religious terms and stories that are infantilizing and subtly insulting to the female gender affect our deepest sense of ourselves, often without realization or direct correlation. So God-talk remains insidious and undermining when it could and should be nourishing and strengthening.

The way we talk about God also reflects, shapes, and perpetuates common theology. It keeps irrational and harmful notions alive—for example, that hurricanes are God's way of killing off non-Christians, diseases are punishment for homosexuality, and school shootings are God's response to people supposedly kicking Jesus out of classrooms.

It is up to us to call it like we see it on traditional, old God-talk: a fallible, human view of God invented in times when people, politics, science, religion, society, and life were very different. It is up to us to update God-talk to reflect what we know to be true today, and use it generously. We can harness the power of God-talk to promote what is healthy, healing, and productive for women around the world. The characteristics of female God-talk include empathy, empowerment, remembrance of women's suffering, and deep thinking about our actions toward others. For instance, on Mother's Day 2013, I prayed before my congregation to our Mother God about all the wondrous gifts of the female aspects of God, and also in celebration of the discovery of Gina de Jesus, Michelle Knight, and Amanda Berry, the women kidnapped in Cleveland by Ariel Castro and held prisoner and abused for more than a decade. You can read it here: http://www.patheos.com/blogs/femmevangelical/2013/05/a-mothers-day-prayer-to-our-mother-god/.

Truly Seek God

For many of us, God was initially taught and defined, rather than encountered and experienced. Or perhaps vice versa—as young children we encountered and experienced God, but the God who was taught to us and defined for us quickly took over. *Do you long to just be with God* and be allowed to accept and explore the God you find in that intimacy, whatever it turns out to be? Do you want to be able to pray without feeling forced to beckon the feudal Lord who waits impatiently in the clouds for us to come bow before a throne? Do you want to be done with the God who is all pomp and power structures? Because of the way God has been traditionally presented in Christianity, making room in our heads and hearts for another reality is something we must learn how to do.

The human mind is built with a powerful ability to create its own sense of reality within which to operate. Scientific research shows that our brains are responsible for not just deciphering, but creating the world around us. We establish our own views and narratives to explain our surroundings and give them meaning. Or, as is often the case, our society or religion has already established the narratives to explain our existence and the phenomena that occur in the world; we assume it's correct and fit ourselves into it.

But this can get tricky as we learn, grow, and change. "The transformation of sense experience into perceptions will draw on prior beliefs: we have an overwhelming propensity to perceive what we expect to perceive," writes Dr. Raymond Tallis in Oxford Journals' *Brain: A Journal of Neurology*.[10]

There is good reason we were made this way. "Associative learning—the conditioning of reflexes and the like—enables us to discover which of our actions influence the future, and indeed, to predict reward," notes Tallis. "Associative learning enables the brain to construct a map of the world. This is essentially 'a map of value,' which intimately ties our bodies to the world around us so that we can respond in the quick and efficient way essential for our survival."[11] The danger is that too often we stay in autopilot mode, ignoring new information while replicating detrimental patterns of survivalist living. We easily get stuck in backward behaviors and self-sabotaging beliefs.

As much as our tendency to replicate patterns has been misused by world leaders and religious powers over time to subdue people and maintain the status quo, there is a flip side. We can reclaim and utilize this knowledge to shift our perceptions and create a new reality for ourselves, as Jesus suggested: freedom for prisoners, sight for the blind, liberation for the oppressed, the eternal jubilee. Our map of value can transcend old-world survival instincts and defense mechanisms and discover new rewards for seemingly counterintuitive behavior that takes society to the next level. Instead of being self-centered, we become community-oriented. Instead of being concerned only for our own benefit and those just like us, we become empathic and thoughtful toward those who are different. Instead of dog-eat-dog, we give others a hand up and a place at the table.

But this all hinges on the language we use, the stories we tell ourselves, our understanding of our place in the world, and our perception of what is real. It requires us to stretch and even break our conditioned responses and assumptions. This is what Jesus did. His presence and proclamations about God's coming realm were constantly stretching the human neurological tendencies to help people sense this realm and see it as good. He told bizarre parables that seemed to describe an alternate universe so counter to society's standards and unintelligible to trained brains that many could not understand the points of these parables. He performed miracles of transformation and healing that make us question how reality truly works. He demonstrated that humanity did not have to be stuck with the way things are. He brought stories to life using vividly strange language and images to help people begin to imagine and practice a different way of being.

Biblical interpretation, Christian doctrine, and religious hierarchies have gotten in the way of Jesus' mission and our understanding of it. For centuries the powers and authorities have been telling us that if we dare to use our free will and let our imaginations run wild, we will inevitably screw things up, and get punished by God. If we step outside the boundaries, respond to new discoveries, or see things differently, we will be eternally damned. This has halted the realm of God; it is not what Jesus described as "the way." In the book *Lean In: Women, Work, and the Will to Lead*, Sheryl Sandberg asks what we would do if we were not afraid.[12] We must ask ourselves what we would believe and what actions we would take if God (or people speaking for God) would not send us to hell. What would you say out loud and what kind of woman would you be, if you weren't wary of lightning bolts, disparaging remarks, or retaliation? If you were not afraid to truly seek, what God would you find?

We do not need to waste time and energy taking down the old historical conduits by which we were supposed to find God: the doctrines, rituals, creeds, hymns, prayers, and stories of Christianity. While we must publicly point out the problems with these, we should look ahead and seek God in ways that support and inspire us. This is how we build something new. We start by recognizing that words, symbols, metaphors, songs, icons, and Bible verses *are not our faith*; they are simply the tools by which people have historically tried to capture human ideas about God and formalize shared religious principles.

We can seek a new framework that allows us to perceive God's real-time movement within ourselves and our world. To do so is crucial at this point in history. We have just begun to awaken to the universal consequences of our long-held belief systems. Religious teachings on the submission and secondary status of women contribute to one in four females becoming victims of domestic violence in the United States alone.[13] Restrictions on access to condoms (due to the belief that God sees contraception and consensual sex for any reason other than childbearing as sin) fanned the flames of the global spread of AIDS, and has ruined the lives of women who are forced to satiate the male sex drive and therefore continuously bear children their exhausted bodies and resources cannot support. The belief that God hates variations on sexuality and considers these an abomination leads to hateful beatings and even murders of LGBTQ people. And we are only seeing the tip of the iceberg that is the global child sexual abuse epidemic perpetrated by the priesthood and protected by the Vatican. We are overdue for new discoveries about who God is and what God does, on new terms. If women today seek without fear of retribution, we will find the God of freedom, peace, and justice—on our terms. As Rev. Dr. Jacqui Lewis, senior minister of Middle Collegiate Church in New York City, put it: "Women must birth a grown-up God that is not co-opted by power-over, cries of war, and oppression. Women must be conscious that our testifying is transformative, shaping a new narrative."

Tell Your Story

Testifying, or telling our stories, changes everything. The Bible, history books, the news, most movies and TV shows, and almost all classic plays and novels frame history and shape our worldviews with a male voice speaking from the male point of view. We are socialized to sympathize with male desire and see everything through the lens of male experience. Only a handful of women have been in the position to create our society's popular narratives as writers, producers, and directors. Even so, in order to be green-lit, female stories often cater to the male sensibility of male-fantasy sexuality, base or demeaning humor, and caricatures of women as objects. A few, like the show based on Piper Kerman's book *Orange Is the New Black: My Year in a Women's Prison,* are pushing the envelope and telling raw stories owned by women and from the female perspective to rave reviews. Women's stories are not "chick lit" or romantic comedies. Women and men alike are hungry for real stories, and society benefits from their insight.

Which is why each of us must authentically testify. Change happens when the world increases its sympathy with the real female plight and gets a clear picture of the consequences if women continue to be treated unequally: hunger, illiteracy, disease, poverty, terrorism. Testifying normalizes our experiences, concerns, struggles, perspectives, lessons learned, and visions of the future. It points the world toward a new way of being. We are creating spaces in which God can move, speak, and act. We are bringing the realm of God that Jesus spoke of, in which women are released from our religious and social-narrative prisons and can take our rightful places.

Talk and Listen to Diverse People

I recently interviewed acclaimed author Reza Aslan about his controversial book *Zealot: The Life and Times of Jesus of Nazareth.*[14] Some Christians were defensive and attacked Aslan for being Muslim and writing about Jesus, even though he wrote the book as an historian and scholar of religions who is fascinated by the life of Jesus. Many suspicious critics failed to actually talk to and listen to him; they would have discovered that Aslan spent his formative teen years as a passionate evangelical Christian, sharing his Christian beliefs with anyone who would listen, and attending evangelical youth camps. Later, in college, he encountered the same cognitive dissonance Eva and so many of us did. Aslan was influenced by a Jesuit priest to explore the religion of his Iranian family's cultural heritage: Islam. Today he is a progressive Muslim, but his wife and mother are both devout Christians whom he deeply loves, respects, and supports. His brother-in-law is a Christian youth minister. *Zealot* is far from being an attack on Christianity by a Muslim; in fact, it is dedicated to his Christian wife and her family, "whose love and acceptance," Aslan says on the dedication page, "have taught me more about Jesus than all my years of research and study."

Many Christian media personalities and religious figures attacked the historical context Aslan brought to the mission of Jesus, even though he is by no means the first to do so; many Christian theologians have too. The fear response stemmed from the fact that the historical Jesus—the one we can see by looking at facts and records outside the bubble of institutional interpretations for Christians—challenges our images and religious assumptions about him. Aslan's work in *Zealot* illuminates Jesus in his natural habitat, recognizing the historical realities of his time and place that would have informed his worldview, words, and actions. This should be helpful and exciting to Christians, not threatening—unless we are already worried about the validity of our religious stories. I am heartened and inspired by how Jesus operated in his context before his memory was turned into a religion. I love how much trouble Jesus stirred up as a social activist. I love that he was not a soft-spoken, docile lamb, but rather an outspoken and often smart-ass political commentator, risk-taker, and offender of the status quo. He was, as Aslan shows in his book, a zealot: a radical with a vision of a different world, boldly and courageously leading a resistance against the powers that oppressed and disparaged him and his people. This changes and opens the way to how we can follow him as women.

Know the Difference Between Religion and Faith

At the beginning of our conversation, Aslan made an important distinction: "Faith is indescribable, undefinable, ineffable," he said. "You're talking about an experience of transcendence, something that literally cannot be put into words. What religion [is supposed to do] is provide the language with which you can express this undefinable experience. And that language is made up of a set of symbols and metaphors. Religion is supposed to be a sign-post to God; the path, but not the destination." I looked back on my own history of worshiping the path—the stories, texts, words, prayers, songs, creeds, symbols, books, and buildings—and realized that these all completely missed the destination: God. I had for most of my life worshiped a male-powered construction of God by worshiping the symbols and metaphors the patriarchy had created and established.

"The problem, of course, is that religions are the product of human institutions," Aslan continued. "And as human institutions, they are [party] to the same socioeconomic and political motivations as any other human institution; and certainly throughout history they have been dominated by men. Not just in Christianity, but every religion. The men have interpreted the religion in such a way to empower themselves, often at the expense of women. It's the same patriarchy one finds in every religion."

Aslan writes about Jesus historically as a prophet, which was the role he took on when he quoted Isaiah to announce what he was going to do about the situation at hand. "Messiah" in Jesus' time and in the Hebrew language meant "the anointed one," and referred to a political and/or religious leader who would do something brave or good to advance the Israelite people. The Jews were always looking for the messiah who would rescue them from oppression and put them back in control of their destiny. Some of us see Jesus as more than a prophet, as God's son or a human manifestation of God. There was a political and cultural phenomenon in Jesus' time of claiming that pharaohs and emperors were the sons of God, born to virgins, so to call Jesus that back then was meant as a slap in the face of imperial rule and authority structures. Some understand Jesus as a cosmic savior of those who confess he is the one and only, true son of God; and yet others find him to be more inclusive and world-changing than that. Whatever way you think of Jesus, Aslan's framing of him is no less true.

"I try to remind people that prophets are not inventors of religion," Aslan said. "Jesus did not invent Christianity, his followers invented Christianity; Mohammed did not invent Islam, his followers invented Islam; the Buddha did not create Buddhism, his followers created Buddhism.

"Prophets are *reformers;* their job is to take the religious, cultural, political, and social milieu in which they live and challenge it, recast it, redefine it," he continued. "And particularly in the case of Jesus, part of that challenge was to try to flip the social order on its head."

Religion is one thing, but our faith is what we live by and how we operate. Our faith makes us prophetic reformers. For feminists of faith, this involves challenging, recasting, and redefining a society that misrepresents, disrespects, and suppresses women. This is holy work.

Reza and I posted a video of our conversation on YouTube, where it received hundreds of thousands of views and ignited passionate debates in the comments.[15] Those who attacked us typically began with the accusation we were leading people away from "truth," defined by unquestioned traditional stories and doctrines espoused by a patriarchal institution (as well as the "scary" fact that we were two people of different religions having a great, positive conversation!). But the derisive maliciousness in defense of the old guard did not come from a place rooted in the real spirit of Jesus. The attacks were not made in response to a thoughtful discussion or different information, but to a perceived threat to a highly structured worldview and the symbols and metaphors that hold its unchecked power in place. Jesus warned that the new reality he introduced would be a big adjustment and a struggle to enter, especially for those who benefitted from the oppressive old structures and those who were spiritually indoctrinated under their spell. The realm of God would be for those willing to risk leaving conventional wisdom, assumptions and expectations behind.

Develop Your Own Symbols and Language

This is not to say that the early Jesus sects and foundations for the church started with the intention of hurting people. There were plenty of freedom and equality-oriented early writings in the Jesus movement, which later disappeared. "It's important to understand that [religious] symbols and metaphors were developed as a means of helping the faithful put the teachings of Jesus into some framework for their lives," Aslan pointed out. He went on to say:

> But that also means they are historical constructs. For example, what the cross meant in the year 340, when these scriptures were about to be canonized, and what it means in 2013 are two vastly different things. Symbols by definition are meant to be malleable; they are supposed to be understood in variable ways depending upon who is encountering them. That's why they matter; that's why they have existed for so long, precisely because of that malleability. So there should not be anything standing in the way of any marginalized group, whether it be the queer community, or immigrant communities, or non-orthodox communities, or women, to reabsorb the symbols that were provided 2,000 years ago and to reinterpret them according to their own needs. That's what they were made for![16]

The symbols were hijacked by influential, powerful men and used to create a structure that benefitted them and kept people loyal to an institution instead of God. Believers were taught to obsessively fixate on the symbols and rituals to help them get to heaven. But as the medieval Christian mystic Meister Eckhart said, "If you focus too narrowly on a single path to God, all you will ever find is the path." Aslan added to that sentiment: "When people say things like 'I believe in the Bible' or 'I believe in Christianity' or 'I believe in Islam,' I get so confused.... God is the thing to believe. The others are just sign posts."[17]

How do you find the God you can fully believe in? Your pathway should mean something to you personally, and make sense to you: words and pictures that are resonant for a twenty-first-century woman. A cross of capital punishment or a violent, male-centric story does not have to be the symbol for Jesus' presence and influence. The language and rituals can be anything that empowers you and makes you feel bold, hopeful, and holy

Take Things Personally

It was August 2008 and hot as hell in my hometown of Birmingham, Alabama. I was visiting from New York City, where I had lived for about five years, to spend time with my family. I had just quit my corporate advertising career, and relinquished the level of success I had worked hard to achieve, in order to go to seminary. The opportunity to study something that truly fascinated me—theology and ethics—had appeared before me like a spring in the desert. While I was not sure what a Master of Divinity degree would mean for a woman raised in the Southern Baptist church, I was sure of this: God had found me in a dry land and was leading me to restoring waters. I had planned to spend the days before I started graduate school drawing from a spiritual spring of sorts: reading and praying, transitioning into the mind-frame of a new purpose, and listening for God's voice, ready to follow.

During the visit, I heard that a prominent evangelical mega-church in a wealthy suburb of Birmingham had called a young graduate of New Orleans Baptist Seminary named David Platt as senior pastor. He was twenty-nine at the time, and his youth was notable. Though I had disassociated with the Southern Baptists long before, I wondered if Platt's hiring meant progress. Maybe this guy would shake up the traditional church format with a fresh worldview and a Gen-X edge? Maybe the Bible Belt would loosen up a notch and let people take a deep breath, get a little oxygen to our brains?

I went to a service the Sunday before I was to fly back home to New York, and the congregation was nominating elders and deacons. Platt preached on the qualifications and expectations for these roles: honor, self-control, reliability, respectability, high character, impeccable discernment, a well-disciplined family, and so on. Then he told the congregation that they could not nominate women, since females were not allowed to hold leadership positions in the church. He insinuated the biblical assumption that women held none of the aforementioned qualities. He nervously reminded the audience that he was just the messenger; it was God's decision, not his. It was by "God's word" that women were restricted.

His argument was based on 1 Timothy 3:1–13, which basically excludes women from leadership by the use of masculine pronouns and the social assumptions of the time. This would be expected among most first- or second-century writings of the Roman-ruled diaspora. But here we were in the twenty-first century; many of the well-off women in the large congregation were corporate executives, business owners, and community leaders, and many of them tithed to the church. Yet they were listening to a young ordained man tell them God didn't believe they could lead with their true strengths in the capacity that was probably most dear to them: their religious tradition.

I wondered if Platt had considered the implications of telling half his congregation that their Creator God thought less of them than men. It didn't seem very pastoral, unless Platt himself truly believed that women were secondary in stature and subordinate to men. In the lesson, Platt also referenced 1 Timothy 2:11–15. Women of the time were to "learn quietly and in full submission," and were never permitted to teach or have any type of authority over a man. The author of the letters to Timothy gives this reason:

> For Adam was formed first, then Eve. And Adam was not the one deceived; it was the woman who was deceived and became a sinner. But women will be saved through child bearing—if they continue in faith, love and holiness with propriety. (vv. 13–15, NIV)

Is this how you view yourself as a woman? Do you consider yourself eternally deceived and responsible for the advent of evil? Do you think repeatedly making babies convinces a heaven-pacing Jesus to save your sorry, secondary ass? Neither do I. But there are a large number of powerful, male religious leaders who still think of us this way. And so did the twenty-nine-year-old senior pastor of an enormous church, who went on to write a national bestselling book. If we think that people with such extreme views about women are few and far between, or not listened to by society, *then* we are allowing ourselves to be deceived.

But then Platt broke from his fundamentalist biblical literalism to insert his opinion that actually, Jesus would save women the same as men. *Well, thank God,* I thought in my best sarcastic inner voice, *especially for those women who are physically unable to have children, or don't choose to have them, or can't find the right person to have them with... But hey, wait, what happened to taking this text literally, word for word? You can't have it both ways!* Platt added that children's education, administrative assistance, or social planning were areas God would surely be pleased to see a lady lead, although I knew that those guidelines could not be found in the Timothy text. I was so angry at his irresponsible manipulation of both scripture and his congregation—not to mention the confused, dashed hearts of hundreds of little girls in the audience.

Equally disconcerting, some evangelical churches in New York City—with famous pastors like Tim Keller—also still restrict the roles of women, and talk around the issue in a way that sounds as if women might be equal, in the same way the Pope "values" women. So not only did I learn that the Bible Belt is tight as ever; I realized the religious oppression of women remains more like a nationwide pair of Spanx, holding people securely in their "place."

But one thing is for sure: that sermon by Platt changed the mindset with which I set off to seminary. I had not been a feminist in a formal way before that day, although I had increasingly strong opinions about women's treatment in society. I realized God led me to visit that mega-church to show me my purpose. David Platt might be shocked to know he helped God move in my life by making me a card-carrying feminist in the course of one half-hour Southern Baptist sermon. In the great wisdom of the movie *Dirty Dancing*: "No one puts Baby in a corner!"

God incited a righteous rage in me that day like I had never known, opening my ears and eyes to the lies disguised as the will or word of God, to the detriment, dismissal, and degradation of half the world's population. Instead of walking away in disgust, I decided to take back my tradition, in my own way.

This all happened three years after Aman and the wild Thanksgiving cab ride. Looking back now, I wonder: What is the difference between a regular person claiming clairvoyance and a pastor claiming to speak unequivocally for the infinite mind of God in a way that limits or harms others? Which sounds more crazy: that a stranger might humbly and graciously suggest a consciousness-expanding possibility; or that a well-known minister in a man-made power position would claim God does not allow an entire gender of human beings to do or be certain things, and demand that it is absolute, eternal truth?

I have had to discern which of those voices, Aman's or Platt's, spoke to me with consideration, discernment, encouragement, respect, compassion, clarity, and good modern sense as a vessel of God; and not as a commander and wielder of some assumption of God's authority. The "crazy cabbie" allowed God to meet me and address me directly through his willing openness, letting God say whatever God wanted to say to me in that moment. It wasn't until I started writing this book that I became curious and looked up the meaning of the name Aman. In Sanksrit it means "peace." In Arabic, it means "trust and safety." It is also the same word for "amen" in ancient Hebrew, meaning "believe" or "I affirm." Aman was right about my future and my voice. Who would have guessed that seven years after that cab ride, I would become an ordained Christian minister myself?

Women can discern the real God through affirmation, not condemnation or doubt. Yet men like Platt hold tremendous influence among Christians, and a powerful religio-political voting bloc. His beliefs affect our ability to get equal pay, to access contraception, to chose our own healthcare, to attain the top levels of the careers we choose, and to fulfill our greater purpose.

I could have left the church that day and thought, "Oh well, what do you expect from a Southern Baptist church? That's their problem. I've moved on." I could have flown out of Birmingham and forgotten about it. But I realized that this matters for all women; whether it happens to me or to someone else, whether it happens on my block or far away. God called me to make it personal, and to use my voice to address it.

As the famous writer, director, and producer Nora Ephron said in a 1996 commencement speech at Wellesley College:

> Don't underestimate how much antagonism there is toward women and how many people wish they could turn the clock back. One of the things people always say to you if you get upset is, don't take it personally. But listen hard to what's going on and, please, I beg you, take it personally.[18]

Believe with All Your Heart, Mind, and Strength

In order to fully believe in God, we must also believe in ourselves. In order to believe in a God who loves us unconditionally and completely, we must be able to love ourselves. In order to believe in a God who bestows upon us potential and purpose, we must also know without doubt that we possess these things. In order to follow Jesus, we must develop our personal agency, affirm our power to choose and act, and take our rightful places. We have to believe we were born with the capability, and have what it takes. We must believe in a God who believes in us too.

Traditionally, we women are taught to love and trust God with all our hearts, while being undermined by that same God's "word." We cannot love and trust God in such a way without being taught and allowed to equally love and trust ourselves. Inevitably, the equation of relationship with God breaks down. Because of this dislocation, we miss true revelations of who we are, who God is, and what must be done in the world. We fail to hear, believe and learn from that still, small voice inside ourselves. We listen to every other voice instead. And just because they are loud, male, and authoritative, does not mean they are speaking our truth, or any truth at all.

It is time to realize the power and value of our stories—or our songs, as Maya Angelou says—and realize God is in them. We were created to reveal God and help bring the new realm, just as a bird was born with a built-in song to sing. A bird desires nothing more than to sing her song; likewise, we were meant to be authentic to ourselves. The institution of religion puts the bird in a cage "for its own good." Living faith, on the other hand, encourages the bird to freely sing its own song for its own good, the good of others, and the love of God. Women's stories have been historically silenced, and we have often remained silent out of shame or intimidation.

But as feminist poet Audre Lorde once said, and many of us have learned the hard way: *Your silence will not protect you.*

When we recognize this, we know that faith is not about one elite group telling everyone else who God is, or ordained men brokering that relationship for us. When we truly know ourselves and our stories, and we begin to recognize our unexpected interactions with God, everything looks different. We can believe. As C.S. Lewis said, miracles are a re-telling in the small letters of your every day experience, the universal truths that apply to us all. This is the faith mission of the modern muse: to inspire new narratives, language, metaphors, and symbols by which God's miracles are extolled.

I recently attended a gathering where the musician India.Arie debuted songs from her album "SongVersation." She said, "Every time I perform, I bring my spirituality out on stage with me." Her voice, lyrics, experiences, stories, passion, talent, and presence with an audience are her spirituality. They are her relationship to, and expression of, God. Yours may look and sound different, but yours also changes the atmosphere. "There is never a time I sing when I don't just bring it all and go there, creating new energy," she said. No matter what naysayers may tell you, your energy and essence makes a difference in the world. The most Godly thing you can do is commit to be fully yourself, tell your stories, sing your songs.

We weren't meant to just believe or tell the good news; we were meant to live it. We work alongside the God who says, *See, I am doing a new thing.*

We are about to discuss, dismantle, and disable the three primary culprits that hold women back: Biblical literalism, doctrinal damnation, and hierarchal control. I will not say across the board that the Bible, church doctrine, or church hierarchy are intrinsically bad or immoral. There are good things about each, when used responsibly and sanely. I do not suggest we throw religion away entirely. What I will suggest is how to understand it differently, and use that knowledge to move forward with a faith that supports your real life. Knowing more about how things came to be the way they are will put them in perspective and create room for what is next. There are a lot of stories waiting to be told, and you are God's modern muse.

DEVOTIONAL: The Wisdom Blossom

And the day came when the risk to remain tight in a bud was more painful than the risk it took to blossom.—ANAÏS NIN

Telling our stories makes a difference—in our own lives and the lives of others. But doing so will come with its share of struggles, personally and interpersonally. You may struggle with your past: the pain of reliving mistakes, embarrassments, disappointments, negative experiences, or abuses. People may dismiss, ridicule, judge, or even attack you when you open up and tell your stories. It is often worth it to be authentic, honest, and forthcoming for the sake of connecting with others and sparking change in an unjust and callous world.

At the same time, trust your judgment. Know that you do not have to share with just anyone in any circumstance. Your stories, experiences, and perspectives are treasures; so keep Matthew 7:6 in mind and "do not cast your pearls before swine, or they will trample them under their feet, and turn and tear you to pieces" (NASB).

Society has always improved when intelligent, empathic, emotionally secure, open-minded people can hear the cause for concern of others, and have the strength to consider another perspective, change their minds, and use new information to push for change. It will take courage and wisdom. You have these characteristics, no matter how vulnerable you feel. Do not let the discomfort, insecurity, anger, closed-mindedness, or negativity of others make you feel less-than, silence you, or stop you. When you tell your stories, no matter what they entail, you do Godly work. But how—by what method, or in what state of being—should a woman of faith struggle to make change, both personally and out in the world?

> She struggles with power, with understanding, with open eyes and with patience. She does not look at the loss; what is lost is lost. She does not [concentrate on] the pain of yesterday; yesterday is gone for her. Only if a memory is pleasant does she keep it before her, for it is helpful on her way. She takes both the admiration and the hatred coming from around her with smiles... She believes that both these things form a rhythm within the rhythm of a certain music; there is one and two, the strong accent and the weak accent.
>
> She keeps the torch of wisdom before her, because she believes that the present is the echo of the past, and that the future will be the reflection of the present. It is not sufficient to think only of the present moment; one should also think where it comes from and where it goes. Every thought that comes to her mind, every impulse, every word she speaks, is to her like a seed, a seed which falls in this soil of life, and takes root. And in this way she finds

that nothing is lost; every good deed, every little act of kindness, of love, done to anybody, will some day rise as a plant and bear fruit.[19]

This is an excerpt from a devotional composed from the lectures of Hazrat Inayat Khan. Khan was born in Baroda, India in 1882; he later lived in Calcutta, and then traveled extensively in America and Europe. He was a classical musician and developed a Western version of Sufism, which he designed to have no barriers of race, creed, or religion; but instead to be a way of life that could enhance all religions. He died in 1927 in Delhi. (I took the liberty of changing all pronouns in the excerpt from "he" to "she.")

For the next week, repeat this mantra just before you fall asleep and as soon as you awake: *She struggles with power, with understanding, with open eyes and with patience.* When you are struggling in whatever way—with telling your stories, with your identity and self-worth, with judgment from others, with the media's attacks on your body image, against sexist behavior in the workplace, with questions and doubts—imagine and know that you can act in your struggle *with power.* We all have struggles; not only with adversities, but also with concepts, decisions, the way things are, the way things should be. You don't have to struggle as the underdog or as a victim, as is often presumed by the word itself. You can approach struggle the way Jesus approached his own struggle against the oppressive circumstances of his people: with the power of ideas and belief in your vision, a stance of compassion and wisdom, the willingness to take risks, the ability to see setbacks as opportunities; and knowing that while the ultimate goal may take many lifetimes, the impact is eternal.

Know that you do have personal power, even if it has been dormant for a time, or even your entire life. Know that you have the strength of those women who came before you and who stand beside you. Know that you have the spirit of a loving and just God who is for freedom, equality, and the opportunity to reach your full potential in the here and now. You can approach struggle with understanding: having assessed a situation, knowing what it will take to make change, and doing it no matter what. You can be confident in your understanding and yet not know everything. You do not have to be perfect before acting. You do not have to be perfect at all, period.

You may not know the answer or even the next step, but trust it will come at the right time. You can engage your struggles with open eyes: never letting a blind spot derail you, seeing things for what they are, and envisioning your role and purpose. And you can struggle with patience.

While others blow up at you, harass you, smear you, gossip about you, or try to intimidate you, you can remain calm, poised, and confident. You can always stand up for what you believe without flinching, with kindness and a smile, and with integrity and emotional and intellectual composure. This is true wisdom.

(Note: You should never concern yourself with patience in an abusive situation, whether verbal, emotional, or physical. If you are being abused, manipulated, beaten, or assaulted in any form, patience is not a virtue; report it to a trusted helper and your local authorities immediately.)

CHAPTER 3

"In the Beginning" Gets a
New Ending

The ultimate authority of my life is not the Bible; it is not confined between the covers of a book... It is not from a source outside of myself. My ultimate authority is the divine voice in my own soul. Period. It is not something written by men and frozen in time. —SUE MONK KIDD

Now, to my mind, the Revising Committee of "The Women's Bible," in denying divine inspiration for such demoralizing ideas, shows a more worshipful reverence for the great Spirit of All Good than does the Church. We have made a fetich [sic] of the Bible long enough. The time has come to read it as we do all other books, accepting the good and rejecting the evil it teaches.
—ELIZABETH CADY STANTON

Why must we grope among the dry bones of the past?
—RALPH WALDO EMERSON

What makes someone like Sue Monk Kidd—a well-known Christian author—ditch the Bible as a religious and spiritual authority? In *Dance of the Dissident Daughter,* her book about her journey from traditional Christianity to female-defined spirituality, she describes a series of awakenings to the stronghold of patriarchy, and a "struggle to wake up, to grow beyond old models of womanhood and old spiritualities that no longer sustain."[1] Mind you, this is a woman who had great success in her role upholding and promoting biblical Christianity. A successful writer and speaker in the religious sphere, she was rewarded and respected for her traditional devotions for Christians.

"I was going along doing everything I 'should' have been doing, and then, unexpectedly, I woke up," she said. "I collided with patriarchy within my culture, my church, my faith tradition, my marriage, and also within myself."[2] She realized that much of her belief about God and who she was as a woman was a male-defined construction with roots in the Bible. Her authentic soul was nearly dead, and she didn't want to see her teenage daughter Ann start to conform, too. The day she walked into the drugstore where Ann worked and heard a man, seeing Ann down on her knees stocking a shelf, say to his friend, "Now that's how I like to see a woman—on her knees," she knew she had to fight the status quo. She risked her career, her marriage, her income, her supportive community, and friendships in the process. But she also reinvented herself and her spirituality—a "resurrection," if you will—and has helped others do the same. When I read her book, even as a liberal theologian with lots of tools in my belt, I felt a sense of relief to hear her say: "It is all right for women to follow the wisdom in their souls, to name their truth, to embrace the Sacred Feminine... [T]here is undreamed voice, strength, and power in us."[3] These female attributes have long stayed undreamed and underutilized because our reality has been formed by our religious beliefs, based on assuming the literal truth of the stories we read in the Bible. The problem is that the stories of the Bible, when attempted to be enacted in real, modern life, do not guarantee healthy or happy endings. They entrap us in rigid narratives that do not fit, and are stifling, abusive, and miserable. Used without knowledge of how the Bible was written and why, they can be deadly.

In his book *The Power of Parable: How Fiction by Jesus Became Fiction about Jesus,* John Dominic Crossan—New Testament scholar, historian of early Christianity, and former Catholic priest—describes the traditional performance of the Passion at Oberammergau in the foothills of the Bavarian Alps. The Passion is a six-hour play depicting the biblical stories of Jesus' last week on earth, acted out word for word by the villagers once every decade in gratitude for surviving the bubonic plague in 1634. Hitler saw the performance in 1930 before his election, and again in 1934 for a special three-hundredth anniversary staging. This was Hitler's comment in 1942, as the German army was pushing toward Stalingrad:

> It is vital that the Passion Play be continued at Oberammergau; for never has the menace of Jewry been so convincingly portrayed as in this presentation of what happened in the time of the Romans. There one sees in Pontius Pilate a Roman racially and intellectually so superior, that he stands out like a firm, clean rock in the middle of the whole muck and mire of Jewry.[4]

When Crossan took a group of tourists making a Roman Catholic religious pilgrimage to see the play in 1960, it was the same exact reenactment Hitler had seen. When he later heard about Hitler's fateful quote, Crossan realized that some of the most dangerous beliefs and actions have come from and been supported by literal interpretations of the Bible as the direct, inerrant word of God. Crossan said of the Passion play, "[As a priest,] I certainly knew the sequence of what happened in Christianity's Holy Week from both monastic liturgy and biblical study. What I did not expect was that a story I knew so well as written *text* was so profoundly unconvincing as enacted *drama*."[5]

Crossan detected the same danger many of us at some point suspect lurks in the literal reading of the Bible, but then set aside in our religious suspension of disbelief. In light of Hitler's comment, Crossan traces back to the biblical interpretations that culminated in the atrocities Hitler committed. In doing so, Crossan realizes how important it is for people to understand that the Bible was written in various literary styles, many of which were not meant and are not safe to be taken literally.

For example, he points out how many holes are left in the Passion story when one sees it actually acted out. This is because it was written in one of the many parabolic literary methods of the time. To wit, he notes how odd the story of Jesus' entrance into Jerusalem is, compared with the rest of the story. There seems to be no good reason for the crowd's sudden, volatile shift from excitedly lauding Jesus with palms as he enters the city, to rejection and violent malice, demanding the Roman governor kill him. This can be attributed to the popular polemical literary style used to write the accounts, which purposefully sets up adversarial relationships and creates controversy to build up to the desired outcome.

Each of the Passion accounts in the different gospels are a little different, and are all used to create one overarching idea about what happened. In the common narrative, Jesus must somehow be unjustly condemned to death on the cross, despite the Roman governor in charge of the decision deciding not to condemn Jesus and washing his hands of it. (Keep in mind, these stories later became property of Roman imperial Christendom, and were taught and disseminated under their that power; they had a stake in the interpretations and perceptions of what happened.) In a well-known story line, the crowds are instead given the choice of whether to sentence Jesus to the cross, and hence, because of the strange holes that do not quite make sense, many have interpreted that the Jews were responsible for Jesus' death.

The ambiguity that worked perfectly as a literary style of the time to assemble a story that ultimately promoted a writer's or editor's narrative purpose and outcome, served centuries later to give a powerful viewer of the Passion play known as Adolf Hitler one more deranged "excuse" to hate and blame an entire race of people. Seeing the stories of the Bible literally dramatized revealed to Crossan how much of the Bible, even outside Jesus's speeches, is parable—fictional story invented for moral or theological purposes of that time. Taken as parable, the logistical elements of any given story do not have to make sense, and so the moral of the story is easily reached and highlighted. But when taken literally as precise details of factual events, parables leave ambiguity, cause confusion, and can pose serious problems; in the case of Hitler, stoking his prejudice and undergirding his evil intentions as he plotted the Holocaust.

In the same way, biblical literalism leads to the inequality, abuse, and even death of women around the world still today. This is why getting our understanding of the Bible right is so crucial to our purpose. We must know it, even if we do not use it ourselves.

Many types of parables were popular during the long span of time over which biblical scripture was written. The parables attributed to Jesus, Crossan notes, had a variation in style and purpose. His were subversive stories of how, in the realm of God, the first would be last, and the least would be greatest. People who were brought into the field late in the afternoon to work would be paid equally to those who went early into the same field to work (Mt. 10:1–16). People who buried their talents, or protected and hoarded their wealth and gifts so that the benefits could not be increased and shared, would be harshly punished (Mt. 25:14–30). Seeds of justice would be scattered, but would not take root where the soil of human hearts was hard and devoid of fertile ground (Mt. 13:1–9). People still find Jesus' parables confusing—not only because the morals are counter to what we are often taught either implicitly or explicitly, but also because the sparse details and strange story lines do not make much logical sense. But these stories revealed important truths about the reality Jesus was trying to get people to see and pursue. The story lines themselves were not the point. If we get wrapped up in literal facts, we do not have ears to hear.

When I was young, I hung on every word of Jesus' red-lettered delivery of these bizarre proclamations and admonitions. Beyond saving believers from hell and promising us heaven one day, I was oblivious to any real vision for humanity in the here and now within the gospel. Later, the ambiguity of the Bible and my own cognitive dissonance drove me to investigate the historical context of the New Testament.

John Dominic Crossan wrote in his an introduction to *A New New Testament: A Bible for the 21st Century Combining Traditional and Newly Discovered Texts:* "[T]o know what is inside [the New Testament], you must know what is outside it. ... You must know what was rejected in order to understand what was accepted. And why, and when, and where."[6] He reminds us that education opens up options and possibilities, while indoctrination closes and denies options. If we are ignorant of the events, ideas, and scriptures that existed before the Bible was compiled and canonized in the fourth century C.E. (centuries after Jesus' death, which occurred sometime between 30–33 C.E.) then we have limited options as far as what to think or do about what we find in the Bible.

For Fear of the Femme

Under a layer of plaster in a chilly cave in Turkey called the Grotto of St. Paul, frescoes dating back to 500 C.E. were discovered. Crossan describes one of these frescoes in which Paul, called Paulos, is depicted reading from a book. Astonishingly, two women are featured as well, one on each side of him. One is a matron with veiled hair, Theoklia, standing next to and a little taller than Paul. Her hand is forming the same symbol as his. It is the Byzantine-era iconographic gesture of teaching and blessing, which is formed by holding up the right hand's fingers separated into two and three, signifying the two natures in Christ (God and human) and the Trinity. Based on the fresco, Theoklia held authority in public, even teaching men in the crowd. She did so right beside, and presumably in conjunction with, Paul— the man who supposedly wrote in 1 Timothy 2 that he would never allow a woman to teach, speak or have authority, especially over men. When the painting was uncovered, it became evident that Theoklia's eyes and her authoritative hand gesture had previously been scratched out of the fresco's surface. It is not surprising that, at some point long ago, someone covered it over with plaster, thinking it would be gone forever.

The other female in the fresco is an unveiled virgin, Thecla. She listens to Paul teach, not outside with the villagers, but from inside the window of a house. They are all three named on the painting, but Thecla's name was smudged out, barely readable. This fresco is one of many clues indicating that, at some point, women were well-known and influential figures within early Christianity, and some people didn't like it. The scripture from which this scene was taken is known as the Acts of Paul and Thecla. It was excluded from the Bible.

The story goes that Thecla, around thirteen years old, hears Paul preaching on celibate asceticism. She is riveted by the meaning of the practice, knowing it is her destiny to serve God this way, but she is blocked by the rules of the patriarchy. Men could decide to practice this lifestyle if they were so inclined, but Crossan acknowledges that once a girl had her first menstrual cycle, "[S]he would have passed, with or without her ultimate consent, from the power of her father to that of a husband at least twice her age."[7] When Thecla's father chooses Thamyris as her husband, she refuses him. "But such a decision—*by a teenage girl*—designates not just domestic disturbance but social subversion," says Crossan. She is condemned to the arena to be mauled by bears and lions. But she is protected by both Christian and Pagan women in the town, and ultimately saved by a lioness who turns against the other wild animals in the arena and sacrifices herself.

Thecla's story is important not only for its focus on the brave will and spiritual endeavors of women, but also because, "[I]f you do not know Thecla, you will not know Paul," Crossan says. "You will not understand the thirteen letters attributed to him and making up half the texts inside the traditional New Testament."[8] Crossan book addresses the infamous 1 Timothy 2:11–12 text used by Platt to prevent his congregation from nominating women as deacons and elders: "A woman must learn, listening in silence with all deference. I do not consent to them becoming teachers, or exercising authority over men; they ought not speak."[9] Crossan reveals what is shocking news to many, but is supported by the fresco: that widespread scholarly consensus based on linguistic studies is that Paul did not write this scripture. The letters of 1 Timothy, 2 Timothy, and Titus, for instance, were most likely written more than fifty years after Paul's death.

Scholars and theologians have long been aware of post-, pseudo-, and even anti-Pauline works. It was common at the time to write under the name of a well-known teacher after his death. Texts were created and circulated using Paul's authoritative name, but these texts respond *vehemently against* Paul's own radical statements on equality among Jews and Gentiles, females and males, enslaved and free people. Even as Paul extended the notion of "God's chosen people" beyond Jews to Gentiles—including social pariahs, such as women and slaves—other forces refused to see them as equal. Doing so would upend their social systems and carefully crafted power structures. So they contradicted Paul in his own name. And he was not around anymore to defend his true beliefs.

"Thecla is the specter that haunts 1 Timothy," Crossan explains. Stories of girls and women being allowed to make their own decisions and disrupt the hierarchy of power that benefitted from the use of women as child-bearing devices, devoid of rights or choices, meant serious social and political upheaval. It would not do to have such heresy espoused and practiced by someone with Paul's notoriety and infamy in starting a new movement, which carried a message of freedom that excited and liberated the masses. If women could (a) make choices, (b) choose celibacy to protect themselves with a religious shield from being transferred to the control of husband overlords, and therefore (c) avoid the business of slave-labor progeny-production, and maybe even get a religious education, then they would obviously rise up.

When Paul said things like, "There is longer Jew or Greek, there is no longer slave or free, there is no longer male and female; for all of you are one in Christ Jesus" (Galatians 3:28, NRSV), he was following the radical Jesus. Jesus included women, even though the canonized biblical accounts are muffled. Like the fresco, unappreciated details were covered over, amended, re-written, substituted, or discarded, which is why the prominent nineteenth-century women's rights activist Elizabeth Cady Stanton warned Christians not to make a fetish of the Bible. It's why, in the Bible, Paul seems to be all over the place in his opinions and positions. But his well-known obsession with celibacy belies the truth. Crossan says:

> All Christians should know how important that challenge of ascetic celibacy was in our earliest traditions—and especially how it proclaimed the right for women to choose their lives despite patriarchal ascendancy. (Today and here we might not consider celibacy as a badge of freedom, but "today" and "here" are not normative for always and everywhere).[10]

When I read Crossan's remarks, I was reminded of a 2012 article in *Marie Claire*, which made it clear how taboo the phenomenon of the unmarried and independent woman still is today. It was a three-part series about "Love and the Single Girl," and the third part, "The Single Girl Revolution," was prefaced: "Putting themselves first and a wedding ring second, a new generation of women fights for their right to be left alone (literally!)."[11] The author, Rebecca Traister, cites über-conservative, sexist shock-jock Rush Limbaugh in the midst of his character assassination of unmarried law student Sandra Fluke when she defended women's right to contraception. Limbaugh berates a female journalist covering the story with the question, "What is it with all these young, single white women?"

"Limbaugh isn't alone in his anxiety about maritally uncommitted broads," Traister says. She gives examples of modern men condemning single women, and then exposes the patriarchy still deeply entrenched within many women who protect their place in the world by vehemently enforcing the old rules, including television writer Tracy McMillan. Her blog post, titled "Why You're Not Married," went viral with its "damning explanations for extended singlehood," including "You're a Bitch," "You're a Slut," and "You're Selfish." When women talk that way about and to other women regarding their hard-won freedom and independence, there is only one thing standing behind it: engrained patriarchal fear and loathing. It seeps into socially conditioned women too.

"What exactly is so threatening about a woman without a ring on her finger?" Traister asks. "What's she done to you? It's not like the failure to marry by 30 is the end of the world." But then she reminds us that this trend marks the end of a male-dominant way of life. It is the end of the world for those invested in controlling to what degree women are understood to be human and autonomous; for those with an interest in subduing our psyches, bodies, options, and decisions under the headship of a husband. It boils down to the need to keep us secondary in status, to keep us believing we have no worth on our own.

Traister says that "[T]he world as we've known it for a very long time—one in which a woman's value was tied to her role as wife—is ending, right in front of us." Women are starting to be recognized as possessing an independent personhood and value, instead of primarily as social extensions of men. I'm reminded of a scene in the film *American Hustle*, in which Jennifer Lawrence's character confronts Amy Adams' character in a bathroom.[12] Lawrence puts her wedding ring in Adams' face as each woman fights for her own dignity from polarized, yet oddly similar, perspectives and positions. Each of their abused, confused (yet desperately determined) identities is tied to the same man; they are both struggling in a man's world that defines and traps them, and also pits them against one another. *American Hustle* was set in the late 1970s–early 1980s. That's not long ago. Reflecting on the difference thirty years makes, we know the development of our individual human value is good for the economy, for business and innovation, as well as for the institution of marriage itself. Traister cites growing numbers of women waiting longer to get married, and a resulting decline in divorce rates.

There are many reasons why it is good for everyone when women are free, whole, and living in an environment of support. But it is scary for the patriarchal powers that be, because, "[I]t's now standard for a woman to spend years on her own, learning, working, earning, socializing, having sex, and yes, having babies in the manner she—and she alone—sees fit." No more submission, servitude, manipulation, and control. Traister goes on to make a shocking observation about our current generations of women: "We are living through the invention of independent female adulthood."[13]

When I think about my life and the lives of my friends, I realize she is right. We would easily miss this truth if we did not step back regularly and survey our histories, share our stories, and connect our dots. Regular women like us are creating, living, and normalizing a new paradigm. We are making different choices, envisioning different futures, bringing a new reality into being. It is fraught with personal uncertainties and tough decisions, and also with attacks on who we are and what we stand for. There are still strong systems of intimidation and humiliation, and most are rooted in a scriptural biblical ethos. The National Football League's egregious mishandling of the Baltimore Ravens' Ray Rice domestic violence case—and many similar cases—proves that, in 2014, the wealth and fame of men playing god on a "battlefield" still trumps the health and well-being of women.[14]

But hidden scriptures that have been found, authenticated, and translated can be useful to shift cultural sensibilities. They remind us that freedom and equality, held to be the values of Jesus, were bubbling up in the beginning of Christianity. In particular, the "The Gospel of Mary," whose main character is Mary Magdalene, shows how the Jesus movement fought for women. It acknowledges Mary's authority as a leader and her close association with Jesus. Yet within her own story, male disciples (including Peter) challenge her, indicating a struggle among them to abide Jesus' leadership on such radical inclusion and respect. She defends herself, but in that culture and time a man had to back her to make her legitimate. Levi speaks up to support Mary, summing up the sins of the patriarchy that still plague us today, and calling it to repentance:

> "Peter, you have always been an angry person. Now I see you contending against the woman like the adversaries. But if the Savior made her worthy, who are you, then, to reject her? Surely the Savior's knowledge of her is trustworthy. That is why he loved her more than us. Rather, let us be ashamed. We should clothe ourselves with the perfect Human, acquire it for ourselves as he commanded us, and proclaim the good news, not laying down any other rule or other law beyond what the Savior said." After he had said these things, they started going out to teach and proclaim. The Good News according to Mary. (The Gospel of Mary, 10:7–15)[15]

According to this account, Peter apparently had a well-known problem with making up rules outside what Jesus taught after he was gone—laws that did not reflect what Jesus believed. *But if the Savior made her worthy, who are you, then, to reject her? Surely the Savior's knowledge of her is trustworthy.* No matter what is said in the Bible, men cannot tell us who we are in God's eyes. We are recognized by the Child of Humanity. Mary's ability to raise discussion and debate among the group "turns the tables on claims like that of the Vatican that women cannot be priests because there were no women disciples," Hal Taussig, editor of *A New New Testament*, points out.[16] There indeed were, but many details of those accounts have been excluded from Christian tradition, as Levi's mention of "the adversaries" might indicate.

The Gospel of Mary also challenges the Roman philosophical duality of lofty spirit and corrupt flesh attributed to Jesus. Mary's message, in which Jesus is known as the "Child of Humanity," is centered around teachings of Jesus concerned with making people more complete and enlightened humans, rather than transforming us into ethereal spiritual beings. Jesus is said to have come in order to make us into *human beings*, and, as Taussig puts it, to tell us "what good news human existence embodies."[17] This changes the purpose of our spiritual practice and our purpose in life, by telling us that our humanness is good news, as opposed to something to escape. This would also challenge the common cultural association of the female gender with a sensual, animalistic, earth-bound, dirty, unspiritual body. Here, Jesus is not teaching condemnation and repression of our humanity to get to heaven, but rather shaping, practicing, and enhancing our humanity to reveal and promote its innate goodness. We don't need to waste time trying to transcend our bodies or our humanness; we are right where we're supposed to be to reach our potential right now.

> The Savior said, "...That is why the Good came into your midst, coming to the good which belongs to every nature, in order to restore it to its root." (The Gospel of Mary, 3:56)

> Mary...said "...Let us praise his greatness, for he has prepared us and made us Humans." When Mary said this, she turned their hearts to the Good, and they began to discuss the words of the Savior. (5:4–10)

> The Blessed One [Jesus]...said..."Beware that no one lead you astray saying, 'Look over here!' or 'Look over there!' For the Child of Humanity is within you. Follow it! Those who seek it will find it. Go then and proclaim the good news of the realm. Do not lay down any rules beyond what I determined for you, nor give a law like the lawgiver, lest you be confined by it." When he had said this, he departed. (4:3–11)[18]

Unfortunately, patriarchal Christendom laid down a zillion rules outside of Jesus' leadership, which is why we need feminism. But Mary's message can deepen the practice of our feminist faith. When I read her words, I am inspired that following Jesus is meant to restore humanity to our true selves. I am inclined to waste no time listening to those who condemn humanity as a whole as depraved, or to preoccupy myself with a mandate to change who I intrinsically am, or to conquer my female human nature to pursue an unattainable tameness. Mary's text is not concerned with other-worldly preparation for the "by and by in the sky." It centers on making ourselves and our lives better in the here and now, which is what women around the world are fighting for. Too often, we women are shamed for not being perfect. Too often, we are admonished with religious fervor to be patient and wait for things to improve.

The Gospel of Mary lets me set my mind to work with what I already have and who I already am, knowing I have the power to make a difference. The intrinsic value of being human is different from typical biblical Christianity; especially for women, since we have long been considered enslaved in the chains of the flesh, seductive and sinful, tied to the cycles of nature; while men have been associated with transcendence, spiritual perfection, higher-minded purpose, and direct communion with God. But Jesus did not buy into any of that. So how did the Bible come to claim that he did?

Canonizing Jesus

Jesus was crucified between 30–33 c.e. The blinding "road to Damascus" conversion of Saul of Tarsus—a Jew with Roman citizenship known for persecuting early followers of Jesus—into Paul the writer of New Testament letters, is reported to have occurred around 37 c.e. Paul did not write his first epistle until about a decade after that vision was said to have occurred, around 48 c.e., and then he intermittently produced letters up until around 56, when Romans was believed to have been written. He later died in Rome in approximately 64–67 c.e., around the same time as Peter. Although the Bible does not mention this, it is a church tradition that both died as martyrs because they were perceived as threats to the Roman Empire.

Back in Jerusalem, there was a another Jewish revolt against Roman imperial rule around 66 c.e., and Rome decimated Jerusalem in 70 c.e. This bloody slaughter of Jews and fiery destruction of the city, including the Temple, precipitated the writing and circulation of the gospels about a sacrificed hero who had already conquered the enemy for all time: Jesus. The Gospel of Mark is traced to around 70 c.e.; it was the first gospel and for a long while stood alone. The writing of the gospels of Matthew and Luke are traced to 80–90 c.e., both using Mark's framework and also diverting from and contradicting Mark on some important elements of the story of Jesus, such as the place and circumstance of his birth. The gospel of John—arguably the most ethereal, spiritual account of Jesus, in which he is presented as Christ, called the Word of God, and the Wisdom who was with God before creation—was written some time between 90–120 c.e., perhaps up to nearly a century after his death.[19]

In the first 500 years of the Jesus and/or Christ movements, there was an extensive selection of literature being used. Although the sayings of Jesus had been written and collected between 50–75 c.e. in what is called the Q source and in The Gospel of Thomas, there was no concept of a New Testament or the Bible yet. Christian pastor, New Testament scholar, and professor Hal Taussig explains the long, complex process of canonization of the Bible in *A New New Testament*. In short, it started with the Roman teacher Marcion's list of what he felt early Christians should be reading in the mid-second century. Marcion thought Paul's writings and certain parts of the Gospel of Luke were the only texts "without error." He nixed the other gospels and parts of Luke because he felt they dwelled too much on the traditions of Israel, Jesus' actual context. The opponents of Marcion retaliated by burning his writings.[20] And so it went back and forth for an extended time among prominent men with various opinions and motivations.

Irenaeus, bishop of Lyons, France, is thought to be the first to use "new testament" as a collective term for Christian writings, in order to distinguish them from the Hebrew scriptures still used to guide early movements. He cited Matthew, Mark, Luke, and John as his preferred gospel texts. He chose four out of the numerous gospel accounts available; not because he considered them the only four of value, but more interestingly to represent the four "corners" of the earth and the wind blowing from four directions. Later, Syrian theologian Tatian got creative and combined Matthew, Mark, Luke, and John into a story called the *Diatessaron*, but the striking differences between the gospels were too obvious and raised questions when they were all brought together.

Between 190–310 c.e., there was no definitive list of Christian texts, but the Montanist sect wrote about new visions and messages from Christ, which caused the higher ranks to claim authority of only older texts and close off any new additions.[21] The Roman emperor Constantine issued the Edict of Milan in 313 c.e., legalizing Christian practice and worship. Some years later, the preferred imperial version of Christianity became the state religion of the Roman Empire, which ignited its worldwide spread as Rome violently conquered and occupied more lands and peoples, conforming them to their culture.

The Council of Nicaea was commenced by Constantine in 325. This was the exclusive meeting during which the church fathers decided how to formally acquire the Jesus movement from its scattered origins. They determined who they thought Jesus was, decided that he would be called "Son of God" like their emperors, and defined his relationship to "God the Father." They also debated and developed their Christology—their vision and interpretation of the nature, person, doings, and teachings of Jesus as the Christ—and began to outline canon law, (the regulations set by ecclesiastical authority to govern Christianity), and its structures, teachings, and churches of the Christian religion. Hence, it went from rag-tag movements of dissidents who denounced Rome, to a belief system Rome defined, owned, and operated.

This spurred Constantine's historian Eusebius to categorize various documents for the new Christian emperor of a nascent, yet sprawling, Christendom. Taussig cites Eusebius' "recognized" texts as including Matthew, Mark, Luke, John, Acts of the Apostles, fourteen letters of Paul, 1 Peter, and 1 John. In the "disputed" category he put James, Jude, 2 Peter, 2 John, and 3 John. In the "spurious" category were the Acts of Paul, the Apocalypse of Peter, and the Teaching of the Twelve Apostles, none of which are in the canonized Bible today. The Revelation to John occurred in both the "recognized" and "spurious" categories, indicating, Taussig says, that this was a list of what was most in circulation and discussion at the time, as opposed to which documents he considered "true."[22]

Taussig notes that, for most scholars, the official moment of birth of the New Testament came in spring of 367 in an Easter "festal letter" from theologian and North African bishop Athanasius to the Christians of North Africa. He instructed them to read the twenty-seven books Western Christians use today as their authoritative "New Testament" scriptures. In 382, Pope Damasus asked the theologian Jerome to start on a Latin version of those texts, which came to be known as the Vulgate. There was no production of one single book of the twenty-seven documents called the New Testament until somewhere between the seventh and ninth centuries.

Of course, the Vulgate could only be read by church authorities who knew Latin; ordinary people could not read it until well after the advent of Gutenberg's printing press around 1440, after which literacy began to increase. This accessibility spurred the Protestant Reformation, the violent split from the Catholic hierarchy in 1517, when Martin Luther nailed his 95 theses about the corruption and abuses of the Catholic Church to the door of the Castle Church of Wittenberg in the Holy Roman Empire. With indulgences and penances, Luther and the reformers insisted, men of God were manipulating and robbing people in the name of Christ; their actions enforced by the same powerful empire that Jesus was killed for opposing centuries before.

The Bible is the biggest bestseller in history, with billions of copies in print. According to Guinness World Records, it is the world's most widely distributed book. The entire Bible has been translated into 349 languages, and 2,123 different languages have at least one book of the Bible translated in that language. This can be either a comforting or a disturbing fact, depending on your view of its contents and how the texts are used by those who read them. Despite its massive popularity, most people have no idea who actually wrote the Bible; why, when, or in what context the texts were written; or how the books were chosen, assembled, and interpreted. But what if Christians were taught the actual history of the Bible? What if we used it differently? Might the edgy, dissident Jesus be invited back into the conversation?

Galen Guengerich, senior minister of All Souls Unitarian Church in New York City, talks about the journey that led him to leave the deeply entrenched Mennonite tradition of his Lancaster County, Pennsylvania, upbringing in his book *God Revised: How Religion Must Evolve in a Scientific Age.* Guengerich was raised in a Bible-based tradition in which generations of his family had served as leaders and ministers, and he reflects on his struggle as a young adult to believe in it: the austere lifestyle, the strict doctrine, the narrow theological worldview. When he headed to Princeton for seminary, the first in his family to attend a non-Mennonite institution, relatives worried he would lose his faith. "This did not happen," Guengerich recalls. "What I lost was someone else's faith. What I began to seek was a faith of my own."[23]

The literal reading of the Bible as the only authoritative revelation of the one true God was a big factor in his decision to move on from his tradition. "I was forced to choose between the facts of human experience and the supposed facts of divine revelation," he explains. "I could no longer ignore the overwhelming evidence that the religions of the book have wreaked needless havoc throughout human history."[24]

"Nor could I accept the biblically mandated subordination of women as a fact that made sense in the world as I experienced it,"[25] Guengerich continues. He could not overlook the atrocities and malicious policies against women and girls around the world, "justified by the belief that scripture, whether Jewish, Christian, or Muslim, is an authoritative revelation from a supernatural God." He goes on to explain:

In this view, scripture trumps everything else, including reason and experience. ...[But] the Bible is a creature of its context... Misogyny was in the water when those religions developed. In historical terms, patriarchy preceded the gender of God.[26]

Many of us were raised with the same view of the Bible that Guengerich eventually rejected. But there is another way to look at it. Elaine Pagels is a renowned professor of religion at Princeton University, a scholar and author who has closely examined the early church. Pagels has studied Christian theological interpretations and ancient texts, both biblical and non-canonical. In her book *Adam, Eve, and the Serpent,* she says that anyone who approaches the Bible humbly and seriously must "realize that genuine interpretation has always required that the reader actively and imaginatively engage the texts. Through the process of interpretation, the reader's living experience comes to be woven into ancient texts, so that what was a 'dead letter' again comes to life."[27]

The Bible is a living word left to us by specific voices within specific groups of our ancestors as a testament to how they perceived and related to God, and how that interaction played out over generations in a certain place and span of time. It only keeps living two millennia later if we give it life by reading it *up against and within our own modern meaning and life experiences.* What lets scripture remain relevant are the universal truths that translate across time and space, not the assumption that everything we find there is literally true.

The Truth about Myth

Truth is a funny thing. It can look different from various angles, and can morph from one situation or set of circumstances to the next. Two people in the same room experiencing the same event may perceive its truth very differently.

This is one reason I love the television shows of the *Law & Order* franchise. A crime occurs and, at first, it seems to have gone down a certain way. The trail to justice seems clear. Then more evidence is introduced, different perspectives are relayed by witnesses, bits of new information come in, and suddenly everything is more complicated. An unexpected twist happens and things look different. The original truth changes to reveal something even more truthful. After fits and starts, a combination of intuition, careful observation, and testing of possibilities becomes actionable. A rescue is made, a life is saved, or someone with evil intentions is thwarted. Justice is sometimes, but not always, served. Yet it never fails that a new perspective on reality comes to the forefront, leaving the characters more attuned to what it takes to serve humanity well.

I especially love *Special Victims Unit*—watching Mariska Hargitay's kick-ass Detective Olivia Benson "get it" after struggling through false leads, incorrect assumptions, tricky witnesses, high emotions, combative authorities, and any combination of distractions and missteps. She is often conflicted, but it always comes down to trusting herself, and being open to the difficulties and complexities of the process. I come away from each episode reminded that nothing is ever black and white.

In our world there is cause and effect, actions and consequences, right and wrong. But none of those are truth. There is always another side of truth to be seen, which may not be obvious until we are confronted with the paradox, or perhaps until we have lived it for ourselves. Because truth is far too multifaceted to be tied to strict facts and figures, it is the impetus for poetry, symphonies, paintings, and films. It is the reason we create art, dance, music, and stories.

This nature of truth was more readily accepted in ancient times, and is a prevalent aspect of the stories of the Bible. Karen Armstrong—former Roman Catholic nun, Oxford graduate, world-renowned religious scholar, and bestselling author—says this is critical to acknowledge. In her book *The Battle for God: Fundamentalism in Judaism, Christianity and Islam,* she points out that modern Western scientific rationalism has forced many to reassess their religious traditions, because those traditions were created for a different kind of society with a different concept of truth. She illuminates this by revealing how *mythos* and *logos* functioned together as complimentary ways of seeking and establishing truths (vs. facts) in the ancient world.

"Myth was regarded as primary; it was concerned with what was thought to be timeless and constant in our existence," Armstrong says. "Myth looked back to the origins of life, to the foundations of culture, and to the deepest levels of the human mind. Myth was not concerned with practical matters, but with meaning. The *mythos* of a society...directed their attention to the eternal and the universal."[28] This is why myth works so well to help us imagine an unimaginable God and explore the most impenetrable spiritual questions. Armstrong explains:

> In the pre-modern world, people had a different view of history. They were less interested than we are in what really happened, but more concerned with the meaning of an event. Historical incidents were not seen as unique occurrences, set in a far-off time, but were thought to be external manifestations of constant, timeless

realities... Thus, we do not know what really occurred when the ancient Israelites escaped from Egypt and passed through the Sea of Reeds. The story has deliberately been written as a myth, and linked with other stories about rites of passage, immersion in the deep, and gods splitting a sea in two to create a new reality... One could say that unless an historical event is mythologized in this way, and liberated from the past in an inspiring cult [in the case of the Bible, the Israelites and Jews in diaspora], it cannot be religious.[29]

Myth makes it possible to bring a lesson, event, or idea worth remembering forward in time, to keep it alive. Myth begot ritual, a communal activity that acknowledges and reenacts the sacred significance and eternal truths of a group. It is about the conceptual takeaway, not literal details or historical facts. Attaching myth to the characters of a specific group of people allows us to tell the stories in empathic, personal, and relatable ways that can be translated over time. The characters of the Bible—some real, some fictional, and some a combination—would not have expected people to read their stories two thousand years later and believe they were supposed to think or behave in the same exact ways. It would be like people in the future watching a few of our current movies and thinking they really happened, believing that those actors lived those lives in real time, and thinking they were commanded to spend their own lives reenacting them using the same morals and assumptions to create the same outcomes. Some have happy endings; others are complete disasters.

But, in reality, our modern characters and story lines are simply meant to create the idea, essence, or feeling you come away with: hopeful, humored, pensive, disturbed, moved. They are about exploring different possibilities and finding out what happens without actually living it out. They make a particular observation or point about people and the world. Our stories are an experience to consider, not a map of the future of humankind. Yet look how we all keep repeating the discrimination, grudges, violence, and wars of the Bible, because we consume it the wrong way.

Myth is meant to allow stories and concepts to be carried by recognizable characters of the past and then passed off to new people and circumstances, as in a relay race. Universal truth about faith, hope, and love can then leave the time capsule of historical context behind (i.e., xenophobia; slavery; oppression of women, homosexuals, and immigrants) and enter a new era with different sensibilities and knowledge. This illustrates why the Bible can (or should be able to) be used by everyone, even though it is a story about the journey of particular generations of one small ethnic group of people with a certain culture and worldview within the greater scheme of things. The story of the Israelites—and their experiences among the cultures of the Middle East, Africa, and Asia Minor; as well as their later infusion with Greeks and others in the Roman-ruled diaspora—is the modern religious text of Western Christians today. Why is that not impossibly bizarre? In some ways it is, because of how some people misuse the texts. But technically it can work, because universal truths must be attached to a group of people from the past whom we can get to know and whose narrative we can follow along with, if those truths are to travel. But we have to take the baton and keep moving forward.

Myth attempts to creatively answer the big questions about life: existence, survival, suffering, death, fate, love, loss, success, failure, and purpose. Myth is the recognition that there are some mysteries of life we cannot solve with logic *(logos)*, complexities we may never unravel, and events we cannot explain without guessing. *Logos*, our knowledge based in rational principles and real-time observations of how the world works, must be placed up against *mythos* to ensure we do not operate irrationally, as if the mythical were absolute. For instance, today we do not live in fear of the return of monster giants called Nephilim produced by the sons of God swooping down and raping women, taking "any they wanted," as in Genesis 6:1–4 (NLT). The beauty is this: myth is the human spirit creatively finding respite and growth in the midst of events and situations that could otherwise paralyze us; helping us keep moving forward, heal, and thrive. Myth helps us conceive and create a new reality. But we must abandon our tendency to superstitiously cling to institutionalized beliefs and behaviors spawned by misunderstanding of myth, and apply the universal truths to our new information and circumstances.

"Myth was not reasonable; its narratives were not supposed to be demonstrated empirically," Armstrong says. "It provided the context of meaning that made our practical activities worthwhile. You were not supposed to make *mythos* the basis of a pragmatic policy."[30] But popular strains of Christianity did, and we suffer the consequences of the extraneous laws we create, just as Jesus in The Gospel of Mary warned us.

Yet myth at its best can inspire and transform us, and be used to flip social and institutional structures on their heads. That's why the prophets, Jesus, and authors of early Christian scripture used it. This makes it a spiritual resource for women: a tool to incite change toward equality, freedom, and wholeness. As Galen Guengerich says in *God Revised:* "In some sense or the other, transformation is the main function of religion. The point of religious belief is not simply to affirm that something is true.

It is to make yourself a better person and your world a better place."[31] The stuff of myth is central to our core universal beliefs about creation, redemption, and resurrection.

Reading the Bible as myth can help us understand biblical stories that do not jive with our knowledge of biology and physiology, our real life experience, or our logic and ethics. We can disempower the dangerous and oppressive stories and raise up the elements that promise new life for all people. We can re-approach the Bible with new understanding and intention as women. The concept of redemption is made real. The epic stories that have the power to draw us to our tiptoes—that allow us to believe in what seems impossible, take risks for the greater good, and adapt to a better reality—these belong to us; they are ours to take hold of and reinterpret. They are not owned by those who traditionally wield them to the detriment of others. The stories of the Bible are indeed not literal, inerrant, or infallible. But this does not make them untrue. It is up to us to hear the message that speaks today, and step in as the voice of spiritual and moral authority in the modern world.

The culture wars began when people started using the Bible to enforce their opinions and will upon others whose differences threatened their worldview or status quo. Anyone can claim or contradict any rule you can think of by pulling out statements and interpretations of Bible stories. The result is mostly to divide and terrorize people. When people sling one cherry-picked verse or quote, they ignore the existence of alternate or opposing ideas elsewhere in the scripture.

I used to think that, to avoid being hypocritical, this would have to apply to my own usage of scripture too—even though I like to pick the parts that are inclusive and uplifting of all people. But Galen Guengerich revealed a nuance that helped me realize *I can and must pick and choose.* He pointed out that choosing which scriptures to believe or act upon is one thing if you consider the Bible to be the literal, infallible, divine word of God. If this is really what the Bible is, then none of us can pick and choose from it, because it is all absolute, eternal, indisputable, and immutable. Even the rape scriptures.[32] Even the parts that contradict other parts— "God's word" is just forever at odds, and so are we. In fact, it's already all over; we are all going to hell if we don't handle snakes at church—a mark of saved believers in Mark 16:17–18.

But choosing which scripture to take to heart is another thing entirely if we do not hold the Bible's content to be the literal word of God. Read as myth, bringing the scripture forward in our own ways for our own times is the whole purpose, it is what the stories were made for. The stories were purposefully written as myth, so actually, we are called to pick and choose what we can use and what no longer works. What we choose says everything about who we are as a compassionate and intelligent modern society.

Burying the Dead, Resurrecting Our Lives

In light of this, I thought back to the Christian devotional books for women I read as a teenager. Stories not meant as modern morality tales were twisted into terrible recommendations of "holy behavior" for Christian women, teaching disempowering ideas I have long carried with me. I once taught a Bible study for women at a church in Manhattan using the suggested book *Esther: A Woman of Strength and Dignity* by Charles Swindoll. Women are exhorted to be cunning and selfless like Queen Esther, who saved the Jews by daring to approach the Persian king un-summoned and request his favor, which could warrant death.[33] Swindoll draws bizarre and dehumanizing conclusions for modern women without acknowledging the reality of the story.

Scholars consider the book of Esther fictional; it is full of historical inaccuracies and is written in telltale early Jewish novella style. In true Hebrew Bible form, it is purposefully written as myth, using ancient oral tradition and shifting details to communicate a larger idea about the precarious history of Israel and the Jews' sense of destiny. The character Esther was a Jew in exile in the Persian Empire around the mid-400s B.C.E., when she was kidnapped into a harem of King Ahasuerus, believed to reference Xerxes I. Hundreds of girl-children were "sent in" to the king (otherwise known as raped). Even if he never called for the girls again, they were confined within the palace walls for the rest of their lives as concubines, never to have lives or families of their own.

The character Ahasuerus makes Esther queen, the position being vacant because the previous Queen Vashti refused to obey his abusive orders. Her breaking point occurred when he summoned her to his drunken buddies' boys' night to "show off her beauty." Ahasuerus punished Vashti for giving all the other women in the land the idea that they could question and resist their husbands' commands. Even as queen, a woman with the audacity to stand up for herself was cursed and vanquished for her ungodly resistance to authority. This was the denigrating position young Esther was chosen to fill, but Swindoll does not talk about any of that. What disturbs me about the traditional Christian interpretation of this story is that we are told with pride and awe that God purposefully inserted Esther into this hell hole to do God's bidding and bring about God's will. Why would an omnipotent God need to let hundreds of young girls get kidnapped and raped so that one of them could be put in position to beg for the lives of the Jews? The idea that God knowingly places women in abusive and dehumanizing positions to carry out a plan is gravely irresponsible—I'd call it evil.

In Swindoll's devotional, in a chapter horrifyingly titled "There She Goes—Miss Persia!" Swindoll makes it sound festive and triumphant, like a musical starring Reese Witherspoon from *Legally Blonde*. He describes the period right after Esther is kidnapped and marinated like meat in beauty treatments for a year "under the regulations for the women," exclaiming: "Look at that! It took an entire year for them to prepare these women to be presented to the king. That's a lot of Oil of Olay and Lancôme, ladies and gents!"[34] *Really?* He goes on to assume what Esther's experience was like:

> The original [biblical] text is colorful, [saying Esther is] "beautiful in form and lovely to look at." Before long she will hear, "There she goes—Miss Persia," And she will win the lonely king's heart. It will be the classic example of the old proverb, "He pursued her until she captured him." But at this point, she knows nothing about palace politics or a lonely king or what the future holds for her. She is simply living out the rather uneventful days of her young life, having not the slightest inkling that she will one day be crowned the most beautiful woman in the kingdom as well as the new queen of the Persian kingdom. My, how God works![35]

My, indeed. Xerxes was no poor, unassuming, lonely king; but Swindoll tries to make that excuse for his misuse of power more than once. The fact he thought Esther was the hottest of all the little girls is revolting, not something for Esther to be proud of, or for modern girls to aspire to. And we have no idea what Esther felt, since a male narrator tells her story. Swindoll asserts these disturbing lessons: "God's plans are not hindered when the events of this world are carnal or secular" *(young girls getting raped and the queen enduring abuse: anything for "God's plans")*; "God's purposes are not frustrated by moral or marital failures" (referring to Ahasuerus' frat boy behavior and divorce of Vashti, which wasn't a marital failure—that was misogyny); and "God's people are not excluded from high places because of handicap or hardship"[36] *(referencing that Esther was an orphan and God used her anyway—getting kidnapped, raped, and held captive was not a hardship, but a compliment to women and a life-long spa day, in Swindoll's interpretation).*

While reading Swindoll's book, I recalled a trauma I had repressed from the age of sixteen. Alone in a dance studio with my older male ballet instructor, he molested me. I thought at the time that if it was his desire, there seemed nothing for me to say or do about it. He brazenly assumed some sort of right to my body that I could not explain, and I had not been taught the critical thinking or sense of agency to stand up to him. Exposing him so he would not harm another girl would have never occurred to me. To get through *my* guilt and shame over *his* actions—a typical irony of the abusive power dynamic—I turned to the only other thing as deeply ingrained in my Christian-girl consciousness as male supremacy: the fairytale interpretations of biblical womanhood that ignore atrocities. I avoided the confusion, pain, and humiliation by imagining this man—who had a wife and baby waiting to be brought to the U.S. from a small, poor Eastern European town—would turn out to be a prince, transforming me into a princess with a happily-ever-after ending. I never told a soul. It took me almost twenty years to realize it was a crime, because, in the Bible I was raised on, it wasn't.

This Bible study of Esther marked the first time I questioned what a male authority figure was telling me the Bible meant. Swindoll (the author) was a senior pastor of a prominent church and chancellor of Dallas Theological Seminary, and because of his authority and influence, has now misdirected countless young women. People like to make Esther's story romantic and fateful, but in the social reality behind this myth, about which the Bible is quite matter of fact, she was a subjugated pawn in the male political drama. She is rightly hailed a heroine, but she is not meant to be emulated, no questions asked, for millennia to come. Bringing Esther forward in a way that panders to makeup, beauty, and pageants forsakes the opportunity to talk about what women actually care about: making the world safer and more supportive for the true needs of girls and women: education, economic opportunity, the ownership of our own bodies.

Texts can open honest discussion of the inhumane conditions endured by women around the world. Instead of recreating Esther's womanhood, feminists of faith should ask, *What would the character Esther want us to do with her myth today to raise up women? Who are the Ahasuerus' and his minions of today, and how do we overthrow them?* True wisdom, Galen Guengerich once reminded me, is not for the faint of heart. Wisdom is creating a new definition of "biblical authority"—exploring our history and bringing it forward with the gospel of Jesus: freedom for the prisoners, release of the captives, sight for the blind, and God's new reality that puts us in our rightful places. We are meant to do something about it.

Imagine New Endings

"Why must we grope among the dry bones of the past?" asks Ralph Waldo Emerson in his essay *Nature*, first published in 1836. Chapter One makes the argument that God still speaks, and rather than rely solely on old stories, we must pay attention to what we hear now:

> The foregoing generations beheld God and nature face to face; we, through their eyes. Why should not we also enjoy an original relation to the universe? Why should not we have a poetry and philosophy of insight and not of tradition, and a religion by revelation to us, and not the history of theirs? Embosomed for a season in nature, whose floods of life stream around and through us, and invite us by the powers they supply, to action proportioned to nature, why should we grope among the dry bones of the past, or put the living generation into masquerade out of its faded wardrobe? The sun shines to-day also, there is more wool and flax in the fields. There are new lands, new [human beings], new thoughts. Let us demand our own works and laws and worship.[37]

There have been strong figures in history who have subversively picked from the Bible's stories and applied universal truth to modern social issues. These leaders put new flesh on old bones and changed the world. Martin Luther King, Jr. is the most famous example of a leader who used scripture's mythical ability to open the eyes of society to systemic abuses, spark the imaginations of communities, and mobilize them. In the most well-known example, he invoked the prophet Amos (5:24) in his "I Have a Dream" speech: "But let justice roll down like waters, and righteousness like a mighty stream."

Black liberation theology is carried forward by visionaries such as James Cone, who brought the exodus and Mt. Sinai traditions forward and reframed them for the experiences of black people in America, based in God's call for liberation of the oppressed and provision for the long, difficult journey into a new promised land of freedom and opportunity. Cone also interprets Jesus' closeness with the poor and marginalized—and his suffering and death—as the identification of God with blackness. By redeeming these stories, Cone reveals a God who would never deny the rights and self-determination of black people, despite claims the Bible supported slavery.

Delores S. Williams wrote *Sisters in the Wilderness*, a landmark in womanist theology that brings forward the Genesis story of Hagar, banished by Sarah to die in the desert after Hagar gives birth to Abraham's son Ishmael. Williams uses Hagar's story to address the history of black women in the language of struggle, slavery, exile, social rejection, sexual exploitation, forced motherhood, and poverty. Hagar's encounter with a God who shows up and promises flourishing for the unjustly used and cast aside shapes Williams' theology. Williams says it is not the death of Jesus that redeems both the oppressed and our violent society, but his life, vision, and ministry. "The cross is a reminder of how humans have tried throughout history to destroy visions of righting relationships that involve transformation of tradition and transformation of social relations and arrangements sanctioned by the status quo."[38]

When I read *Comfort Woman* by Nora Okja Keller,[39] I was astounded I had not been taught about the atrocities Asian women endured at the hands of soldiers during World War II. The Empire of Japan provided a corps of prostitutes for the Japanese soldiers by kidnapping girls from Korea, China, and the Philippines. They ripped them from families or tricked them into traveling for "employment," then held them in faraway camps under threat of death. They were called "comfort women" because they were used by soldiers for sexual entertainment and stress relief. There were "comfort stations" in many of the Japanese-occupied territories, such as Burma, Thailand, Malaysia, Taiwan, Indonesia, and Vietnam. *Comfort Woman* is the harrowing story of a Korean refugee's abuse in the camps and eventual escape. It describes her daughter's slow realization of her mother's unmentionable past and the trauma that tormented her. Today there are groups of women who, with courage and strength, make it their mission to keep their horrifying personal stories at the forefront of cultural memory, so that no one forgets and it never happens again.

Elsa Tamez, editor of *Through Her Eyes: Women's Theology from Latin America,* says Latina women must develop "theological and biblical tools to tear out by the roots the sources of their marginalization."[40] The authors of the anthology seek echoes of female voices in the Old and New Testaments, giving them new meaning in the Christian context as well as other Latin American spiritual contexts. This includes Candomblé, an Afro-Brazilian melding of African and Catholic traditions and practices in which women are the standard religious leaders. In the Foreword to *Through Her Eyes,* Delores S. Williams writes:

> Biblical interpretation involves a new process,..."a faithful and renewed rereading"...which allows silence [the typical biblical condition of women] to become a point of departure for scriptural exegesis [critical interpretation of a text]. This new process of rereading can yield interesting discoveries about ministry—about the difference between biblically situated male and female models of prophetic ministry. Wholesome views of a woman-identified

God come to the surface of Latin American women's theology, challenging the overwhelmingly androcentric character of the understanding of God present in much of the theology written by Latin American men. The trinity is reinterpreted from a female perspective giving women the right to stay in the church as they "call on God using feminine appellations...," still affirming the Good News of Jesus Christ.[41]

Emerson said: "Every [person's] condition is a solution in hieroglyphic to those inquiries she would put. She acts it as life, before she apprehends it as truth" (female pronouns mine).[42] Only what we test by living and find to be life-giving do we bring forward. Using our female condition, experience, imagination, wisdom, suffering, and redemption, we bury the dead letter and resurrect the living word.

DEVOTIONAL: Passion Prophet

Ezekiel became a prophet while in exile in Babylonia, to which he was deported in 597 B.C.E. King Jehoiakim of Judah had rebelled against Nebuchadnezzar, his overlord in the Babylonian rule of Syria-Palestine, hoping Egypt would come to his aid. Instead, Nebuchadnezzar laid siege to Jerusalem. He installed a new king and deported the then-deceased Jehoiakim's successor Jehoiachin, along with the former royal family and the military, political, and religious leaders—including Ezekiel, who worked in the lineage of his priestly-class family. Katheryn Pfisterer Darr, scholar and professor of Hebrew Bible, explains in the *Women's Bible Commentary* that Ezekiel "struggled to convict his people of their sinfulness, to justify God's actions, and to articulate a vision of Israel's future."[43] This is the classic prophetic formula. Religion and politics were inseparable, and everything that happened within or to Israel was assumed to be God's will—either benevolent provision or violent punishment.

In one scene, God takes Ezekiel to see a valley full of dry bones and asks the prophet if they can live. God tells him to speak to the bones about their future and divine purpose and see what happens. He obeys, God breathes life into them, and soon a vast army of enfleshed people stands before him. Ezekiel perceives the people as an army because this is a political vision couched in spiritual terms. It symbolizes the resurgence of Israel; it was the author's way of saying they would take back Jerusalem and rule themselves under their God Yahweh again. It was a message to uplift a nation under foreign rule; a prophetic story of redemption that had not yet happened. It envisioned a day when the Israelites would take their rightful place.

Even though the author of Ezekiel was one of the worst purveyors of the political imagery of women taking the brunt of the violent and misogynist wrath of God (just read through the whole book), we can reject that while bringing his more imaginative visions forward in helpful ways.

First, read the scripture below. (Notice that God calls the prophet Ezekiel the same name Jesus, centuries later, uses to refer to himself: Son of man. Growing up, Jesus would have heard the scroll of Ezekiel read out loud in the temple.)

> The hand of the LORD was on me, and he brought me out by the Spirit of the LORD and set me in the middle of a valley; it was full of bones. He led me back and forth among them, and I saw a great many bones on the floor of the valley, bones that were very dry. He asked me, "Son of man, can these bones live?" I said, "Sovereign LORD, you alone know." Then he said to me, "Prophesy to these bones and say to them, 'Dry bones, hear the word of the LORD! This is what the Sovereign LORD says to these bones: I will make breath enter you, and you will come to life. I will attach tendons to you and make flesh come upon you and cover you with skin; I will put breath in you, and you will come to life. Then you will know that I am the LORD.'" So I prophesied as I was commanded. And as I was prophesying, there was a noise, a rattling sound, and the bones came together, bone to bone. I looked, and tendons and flesh appeared on them and skin covered them, but there was no breath in them. Then he said to me, "Prophesy to the breath; prophesy, son of man, and say to it, 'This is what the Sovereign LORD says: Come, breath, from the four winds and breathe into these slain, that they may live.'" So I prophesied as he commanded me, and breath entered them; they came to life and stood up on their feet—a vast army. Then he said to me: "Son of man, these bones are the people of Israel. They say, 'Our bones are dried up and our hope is gone; we are cut off.' Therefore prophesy and say to them: 'This is what the Sovereign LORD says: My people, I am going to open your graves and bring you up from them; I will bring you back to the land of Israel. Then you, my people, will know that I am the LORD, when I open your graves and bring you up from them. I will put my Spirit in you and you will live, and I will settle you in your own land. Then you will know that I the LORD have spoken, and I have done it, declares the LORD.'" (Ezek. 37:1–14, NIV)

It is important that we understand any biblical passage first in its original context. I recommend the *Women's Bible Commentary*. This is how we learn the historical reality of the story and keep scripture from being used in disingenuous and dangerous ways. We have to know what the author was addressing and why, and what the message meant to the people it was written for in historical and literary context. Then we can do responsible re-imagining of scripture.

With the top tier of Israel in exile and their land ruled over by foreign power, it seemed Israel was dead and buried. The people's hope had dried up. Only the scattered bones of history were left to litter the valley, a clear symbol of a low point. The author has God walk Ezekiel back and forth to survey the scene and ask if life is possible for these remnants. Ezekiel defers to God, but God insists he do the work: "Speak to these bones and prophesy." The attention of a human being is required to make something happen. Once the prophet realized that, spoke up, and took action, miraculous things began to happen.

How does this story and its implications correlate to the lives of women around the world? How about your life? At first glance, in the original biblical text, it seems there is just a male God and a male prophet. But there actually is a woman who touches the story and brings it alive: you. God shows up, works with our mindsets, teaches us what we need to know, leads us to the right place at the right time, and shows us visions. We examine the situation, set an intention and speak into it. Of course, the author put his own desire to return to Israel and take back the land into God's mouth. But we can do the same for our own benevolent dreams, without bloodshed.

So, let's bring it forward. What if God showed you the same vision today? What if you put yourself in Ezekiel's place, not as a biblical prophet in ancient times, but as the modern woman you are? What would God's voice sound like? What would be her demeanor? Would you hear her in your mind, feel her in your gut? Would you pray her into presence, detect her in a person who says something special to you, or would she appear out of the blue? What words or gestures would she use? How would you feel, physically and spiritually, in her presence? Imagine God shows you a place where there is dried-up hope and scattered, inanimate remnants of life. She asks you whether the bones can live; she tells you the answer is up to you. She asks you to speak into this place, to act upon it with the special insight and power she has vested in you.

How would your view of yourself shift in light of her communion with you? How would having a vision placed in your heart and an important task placed in your hands make you see yourself and your life differently? By regularly tapping into this, you can recognize your interests, desires, talents, passions, and dreams as God's voice in your soul. No one else can tell you what you're meant for. Know that your personal valleys and struggles can be used to enhance the lives of others and improve the future. Know that your own resurrection into new life at every stage of your history, present, and future changes the world.

Maybe it is a homeless shelter in your neighborhood or an underfunded school that needs creative attention. Maybe it is a group for pregnant teens that needs an empowerment element, or the protection of the environment to provide for generations to come. Maybe it is people in a community that is oppressed politically and socially that you want to help raise up in your sphere of influence, to be a part of their "army." There are so many valleys in our world where dry bones lie waiting to be spoken to, to have life breathed into them, to rise up from their graves. People need to be made to feel whole and human again, to be respected and believed, to live in a world that offers hope. Whatever the details, your purpose is to work alongside God to make it so. Resurrection is not just for Jesus, it is an invitation to us all. Women included. You, especiallly.

CHAPTER 4

Truth and Other Lies

Woman's degradation is in man's idea of his sexual rights. Our religion, laws, customs, are all founded on the belief that woman was made for man.
—ELIZABETH CADY STANTON

Do not...give a law like the lawgiver, lest you be confined by it.
—JESUS, *THE GOSPEL OF MARY*

Your time is limited, so don't waste it living someone else's life. Don't be trapped by dogma—which is living with the results of other people's thinking. Don't let the noise of others' opinions drown out your own inner voice. And more important, have the courage to follow your heart and intuition. They somehow already know what you truly want to become.—STEVE JOBS

It was fall of 2005. I had moved to New York City from Alabama less than a year before and the transitions were stressful: acclimating to the pace, getting lost in subways, keeping up with a demanding new job, breaking up with a boyfriend, finding reliable new friends, and adjusting to expensive Manhattan life. Under the circumstances, I was feeling exhausted on that crisp late-September evening. When I finally left the office, I ducked into a little corner spa.

My eyes were closed and my head was relaxed against the back of my seat while my freshly painted fingers and toes rested in the drying machines. It felt good to close my tired eyes and be quiet and still. I heard a manicurist direct another client to the dryers next to me, then felt the person sit down close by. A minute or two passed. Then a female voice whispered, "Excuse me, miss?"

I know she's not talking to me. "Miss? I am so sorry to disturb you." Had my purse spilled on the floor? I opened my eyes to see a very professional-looking woman drying next to me. She was wearing designer everything—what I would imagine to be the uniform of an executive at Vogue. She seemed out of place in this inexpensive chain salon. She smiled apologetically.

"I actually sat here for a minute trying to fight this, but I need to tell you something." Still the polite Southern girl, I raised my eyebrows and curled my lips in a replica of a patient smile that invited her on. "This is going to sound so crazy," she warned with a furrowed brow, "but the moment I sat down next to you I felt this energy, and God pressing heavily on me to give you a message."

God, huh? My expression must have told her I didn't care anything about her weird message. She got my vibe. "Look, I'm not trying to sell you on anything religious, but I think you really need to hear this." I stared at her blankly. If she received messages, shouldn't she already know I was mere months out of the Bible Belt? Didn't she know that I still thought messages from God only came from bonafide biblical prophets and those magical men behind the pulpit? If anyone would already know what God wanted me to know, it was me: the born and raised evangelical Christian. She obviously had no idea how thoroughly and completely I thought I already knew God. I watched her make the decision in her head; it flashed across her face. Instead of backing off, she dove straight into a hectic monologue. I will never forget what she said. It went like this:

> Look, you've always thought you have to be exactly what others expect. Your obedience to this ties you down and holds you back. You think you will disappoint people if you break away or make them mad if you speak your truth. Well, you probably will. But your whole life, people have tried to overpower your sense of self, your sense of direction, your dreams, and your decisions. But, deep down, you know who you are. You've always been pretty frustrated, but you are finally starting to let it come through and drive you. Just let it happen, trust it. You are beginning a journey that you must take to find your voice, and you have to learn how to believe in it and use it. You have something to say; it is something that must be said, something that people need to hear.

She finally took a breath. "Um," I laughed a little exasperated sigh. "I'm just tired and trying to relax. Thanks, though." I leaned my head back and closed my eyes again, shaken at her insight and desperate to disengage.

"Hey, I get it. It sounds nuts," she said with a hint of embarrassment and a surprising amount of empathy in her voice. I cracked my eyes to give her another look. She was spraying a finishing oil on her fresh manicure so it wouldn't smudge. She had the shiniest black hair I'd ever seen—an amazing head of ringlets like a glistening, dark halo. She slung her Gucci bag over her shoulder, checked her nails, and noticed my gaze.

"I hope you'll think about what I said," she chirped. "Good luck with everything." I managed a little wave. I was the last customer in the salon. I sat there with my eyes wide open until it closed.

Apple Computer co-founder Steve Jobs famously warned people against living someone else's prescribed life, and living with the consequences of other people's thinking. It's a good thing he felt that way, or the world wouldn't be accessible from a little glass screen in our palms. His quote at the beginning of this chapter makes good business sense in the world of invention, revolutionary technology, and entrepreneurial innovation. The ability to take risks, break free of expectations, and leave old thinking behind are key to success. His statement is also a good spiritual rule for women when it comes to how to understand and deal with religious doctrine.

Jobs called it dogma, but they are closely related. Dogma is prescribed doctrine proclaimed as unquestionably true by a particular group. It is defined as an official system of principles or tenets concerning faith, morals, and behavior—authoritatively set, for example, by the church.[1] It is an established belief about the order and nature of things. Often it is constructed around a dichotomy of good and evil.

Doctrine takes dogma a step further by a process of formal teaching. It is defined as a particular principle, position, belief system, or policy that is taught or advocated, for instance, by a religion or government. It is the term for the teachings themselves, individually or collectively.[2] There is value in teaching, knowing, and remembering our traditions, being raised and rooted in something of meaning. Yet there is danger in getting trapped in a worldview that deifies the masculine, practices power-over, sanctions or overlooks violence, and propagates the belief that everyone different is going to hell. Unspoken religious rules are deeply ingrained in social structures, even though we often do not fully understand what we believe or why. The system seems much bigger and more powerful than we. But God is much more expansive than doctrine.

Indoctrinating God

Christian doctrines have countless names and versions in various traditions. Let's see... There is the doctrine of purity, which condemns sex outside the institution of marriage. There is the complicated doctrine of salvation, called soteriology, which begins with the assumption that the human condition is utter sinfulness. This corrupt nature is said to be redeemed by God's sending of Jesus as savior to live a perfect life and shed his blood on the cross to save us from the penalty of our sin, granting us eternal life if we believe. There are numerous variations on how one comes to receive salvation: salvation by grace, salvation by works, salvation by faith. There are doctrines of predestination and election that try to explain why, if God knows what everyone will do with their free will before they do it, everyone doesn't end up confessing belief in Christ and getting saved? This doctrine answers that God predetermined the eternal destiny of some chosen people to salvation, while abandoning others to eternal damnation for their sin. Nice.

There are also doctrines built around regulating human behavior, such as the teaching that contraception use is sinful and immoral because it frustrates a divine plan. There is doctrine against homosexuality. There is doctrine about the Eucharist (or communion): taking wine and bread in remembrance of Jesus' Last Supper—during which some believe the wine and bread is transformed into the actual blood and body of Jesus—and exclusive rules about who can or cannot participate. There is doctrine about heaven, hell, purgatory, and the human fear of being "left behind" during an anticipated second coming of Jesus and final resurrection of Christians, about which there is extensive doctrine to map the culmination of the cataclysmic, apocalyptic return of Jesus.

These are some incredibly broad brush-strokes on just a few of the hundreds of doctrines across Christian tradition. It all gets extraordinarily technical—particularly in traditions with elaborate confessional statements—and weaves a dense web of regulations and caveats such as "double predestination," "reprobation," "active decree," "passive foreordination," and "equal ultimacy." At some point it makes me laugh, and then sometimes cry. It may keep people going through the motions and obeying the powers that be, but it drowns out our ability to hear the still, small voice. It smothers and kills the sense of ebullient life we are searching for when we seek God. It keeps us face-planted on the path littered with stuff we make up that never gets us to God.

Doctrine also tends to get confused with the gospel. Doctrine is not the gospel; it came into being well after Jesus was gone. A great deal of doctrine was conceived by the powers of the Roman Empire to establish exactly what the authorities wanted everyone to agree to believe as they engaged with the new state religion and as Rome ripped through the world conquering and subduing other cultures and colonizing their people. So doctrinal staples tend to contain ancient nationalistic thinking with echoes of propaganda.

From Lowly Zealot to Sovereign Lord

Take the Nicene Creed, which outlines the mainstream definition of correct belief for large numbers of Christians. It was created in 325 C.E., when the first ecumenical council met in Nicaea (present-day Turkey). A group of almost 2,000 bishops from the various lands controlled by Rome convened to resolve theological and philosophical differences among them. It was contentious when it came to Christology, since the debate over whether Jesus should be human or divine had caused a lot of drama amongst the educated elite. Eventually they adopted the Nicene Creed and gave it to Constantine; making it the first official, sanctioned outline of Christian orthodox beliefs. In 325, they developed and settled upon this statement as definitive Christian belief:

> We believe in one God, the Father Almighty, Maker of all things visible and invisible. And in one Lord Jesus Christ, the Son of God, begotten of the Father (the only-begotten; that is, of the essence of the Father, God of God), Light of Light, very God of very God, begotten, not made, being of one substance with the Father; By whom all things were made (both in heaven and on earth); Who for us men, and for our salvation, came down and was incarnate and was made man; He suffered, and the third day he rose again, ascended into heaven; From thence he shall come to judge the quick and the dead. And in the Holy Ghost. (But those who say: "There was a time when he was not"; and "He was not before he was made"; and "He was made out of nothing," or "He is of another substance" or "essence," or "The Son of God is created," or "changeable," or "alterable"—they are condemned by the holy catholic and apostolic Church.)

Nice little jab at the hesitant or dissenting debaters inserted there at the end, right? Well, by 381, the First Council of Constantinople had changed the creed significantly. The powers of the time added a great deal of explanatory new detail, including the decision that Jesus had existed in heaven before living on earth, and was born by a divine-human conception and virgin birth, which were cultural myths that already existed and had a particular political connotation well before they were applied to Jesus. It went something like this (I've italicized the changes):

> We believe in one God, the Father Almighty, Maker *of heaven and earth,* and of all things visible and invisible. And in one Lord Jesus

Christ, *the only-begotten Son of God, begotten of the Father before all worlds* (æons), Light of Light, very God of very God, begotten, not made, being of one substance with the Father; by whom all things were made; who for us men, and for our salvation, came down *from heaven,* and was incarnate *by the Holy Ghost of the Virgin Mary,* and was made man; he *was crucified for us under Pontius Pilate, and* suffered, *and was buried,* and the third day he rose again, *according to the Scriptures, and ascended into heaven, and sitteth on the right hand of the Father;* from thence he shall come again, *with glory,* to judge the quick and the dead; *whose kingdom shall have no end.* And in the Holy Ghost, *the Lord and Giver of life, who proceedeth from the Father; who with the Father and the Son together is worshiped and glorified, who spake by the prophets. In one holy catholic and apostolic Church; we acknowledge one baptism for the remission of sins; we look for the resurrection of the dead, and the life of the world to come. Amen.*[3]

As you can see, a lot was debated and created over a half-century of discourse about the conflicting gospel accounts and other texts, and the answers of one group of powerful men were crafted into doctrine. Irrefutable claims of absolute, eternal truth materialized in the context of an imperial religion, making clear what and whom the public were to loyally support with religious fervor. They were political statements about the eternal rule of Rome couched in spiritual language, in the style of Jesus—but now reversed, revamped, and stamped with a seal of approval by the Roman emperor (by now Theodosius, who followed Constantine). And they silenced the zealot by making Jesus Lord of it all.

In his book *Not Every Spirit: A Dogmatics of Christian Disbelief,* Methodist minister and theology professor Christopher Morse reveals the historical absurdity of this. One of the most common doctrines of Christianity is that of Jesus as Lord. It is a contemporary, widespread title used to indicate the divinity of Jesus and the belief that he rules as the heavenly king. It is also still a common confession in the doctrine of baptism, where people who "accept" Jesus are washed with water as a cleansing of sin, and as a rite of passage and acceptance into the church. "Probably for most [the ritual of baptism and title of Lord] seem quite removed in meaning from anything currently political," Morse observes. He goes on:

But the term "Lord" had a secular denotation in the Roman world. Only Caesar [the Roman emperor while Jesus was alive and conducting his mission] preeminently could be Lord. The loyalty oath, the pledge of allegiance, throughout the empire was expressed in the words *"Kyrios Kaisar"* ("Caesar is Lord"). Baptism [like that of John the Baptist] in such a social environment was in part a radically political act, for the confession "Jesus is Lord" represented a subversive claim. Entailed in the faith that Jesus was Lord was the disbelief of Caesar as Lord.[4]

A few centuries later, the same empire that had given Jesus the death penalty for those same reasons, and demolished Jerusalem over religio-political uprisings, now claimed Jesus their own. They made it sound as if his death "under Pontius Pilate," the Roman governor of the occupied territory of Judea, where Jesus operated, was purposeful, even divinely ordained. Why else would they have previously killed the one they now deemed their own Lord of salvation? They gave him a throne at the right hand of God, and vested in him the power of ultimate judgment over the nations of the world, in a (Roman imperial) kingdom that would have no end—all conveniently based in one holy catholic and apostolic Church developed and sanctioned by the emperor. The Roman Empire could not intimidate or kill enough of the little oppressed Jesus groups who had nothing to lose, even as the Romans staged their world domination. They could not squash the sticky tentacles of movements for freedom, equality, dignity, and liberation in Jesus' name. So they took his name.

How interesting for us to employ today in our context. Christians have to create even more explanatory doctrine for the symbolism, imagery, language, and rules to make any sense in their leaps from ancient to imperial to feudal to modern times. From the Dark Ages through the Enlightenment, from East to West; and still the doctrine survived to subdue and defuse women and girls in the twenty-first–century mega-churches of the American suburbs. By way of its unquestioned acceptance and sheer ubiquity, traditional Christian doctrine makes us believe it has definitively captured and encoded absolute truth. But Morse points to a quote from Leo Tolstoy in Tolstoy's *Confession*: "I have no doubt that there is truth in the doctrine; but there can be no doubt it harbors a lie; and I must find the truth and the lie so I can tell them apart."[5]

Schooled or Fooled?

Lily Rothman's November 2012 article in *The Atlantic* called "A Cultural History of Mansplaining" traces the phenomenon of "mansplaining" back to at least 1776, even though the term was not coined until 2008. I would argue it goes back much further. Mansplaining occurs when a man takes it upon himself to explain something—particularly to a woman—"without regard to the fact that the explainee knows more than the explainer."[6] Or, as described when Dictionary.com did an exposé on the popular new word, it is the observation that many people of the male gender generally feel absolutely confident and comfortable explaining things that they do not know anything about. To add insult to assumption of ignorance, mansplainers feel free to explain something to a woman who has actually studied, invented, or personally experienced whatever it is. And society grants men unquestioned permission to do so because of their gender.

Rothman wrote the piece during the 2012 election season, when Congressperson Todd Akin spouted falsehoods on national television about female biology and his bizarre opinion of what is "legitimate rape." Around the same time, a couple of Presidential and Vice-Presidential candidates told the nation's women that all-male panels should be dictating when, why, and how we have access to birth control, and what kind we can have. But Rothman says the word "mansplain" was actually generated in 2008 in response to an article Rebecca Solnit wrote in *The Los Angeles Times* that went viral, called "Men Explain Things to Me," in which she recounts the time a man explained a book to her without acknowledging that Solnit herself wrote it.

But Rothman goes back to an important moment in 1776, when John Adams "mansplained the need to make husbands the legal masters of wives." (Yes, *that* John Adams—thank God that did not end up in the Constitution!) His intelligent wife Abigail wrote him a letter pointing out that if men had complete control over their wives under the law, then many would abuse them and use them like slaves. Of course, many already did, but this would make it officially legal and hence formally moral and defensible in the eyes of the community, with no recourse for women. She suggested that it was also unfair for women to be held under such coercion impressed by a law-making body in which our gender had no representation. Rothman reveals John's response to Abigail:

> Depend upon it, we know better than to repeal our masculine systems. Although they are in full force, you know they are little more than theory... We are obliged to go fair and softly, and, in practice, you know we are the subject. We have only the name of masters, and rather than give up this, which would completely subject us to the despotism of the petticoat, I hope General Washington and all our brave heroes would fight.[7]

Yikes, he's going to pull out the army and start a war over women not wanting to be legally subject as property to their husbands? He condescends in an attempt to convince his wife that men are masters in name only and really have no power over women—even though women did not have a vote or any personal rights, could not get an education, did not own property, were not seen as suitable hires, nor were women generally able to support themselves. Oh, and the man was the head of the woman, so he also commanded the household. Surely John Adams was intelligent enough, as a founding father, to know that naming creates reality, so if man is called "master" and woman is called "subject," an immediate power disproportion is established. "Obliged to go fair and softly"? It was well known and socially accepted that men regularly beat and verbally scourged their wives to keep them in their place. Obliged or not, history proves that most powerful men have seen fairness and logic only from their own perspectives, to the detriment and oppression of women.

Adams invokes the image of the badgering housewife and her "subject" husband who is forced to...I don't know; what did she have the power to demand? Seeing as men were out getting educated, working the economy, creating the rules, running the country, and making all the big decisions that would directly impact all womankind for the foreseeable future. Abigail astutely mentions a legitimate concern and she is manipulatively accused of "petticoat despotism"—the eighteenth-century version of being called a "man-hater" today, simply for pointing out injustices and abuses committed against women.

I especially love that Adams admits that "our masculine systems...are in full force," but then tries to tell her, *Oh, sweetheart, but you know that's just in theory* (fingers crossed behind back). He mansplains to her that everything she knows to be true based on her firsthand observations (men are cruel to their wives) and experiences (I am uneasy that a powerful all-male group that does not represent me by vote could make such a terrible, critical decision about my life) is really just a figment of her imagination. He mansplains that her logic is not a correct assessment of the "facts." He tells her, as Rothman writes, "that he knows better than she does about the experience of being a wife."[8]

The Pope's deceptive statement (mentioned earlier) that "women are to be valued, not clericalised" proves that mansplaining to keep women out of law and doctrine is alive and well. To be frank, a lot of Christian doctrine is historical mansplaining about God. Take Tertullian, an early church father from the Roman-controlled province of Carthage in Africa during the second and early third centuries. He was thought to have been a lawyer, but after his conversion to Christianity he gravitated to apologetics [the defense of a religious position], and inspired Tertullianists and basilicas full of fledgling Christians. He was the first Christian author to produce a whole corpus of widespread Latin Christian literature. He interpreted Genesis 3 as reason to inform his "sisters in Christ" that even the best of them were as dirty and devilish as he believed Eve to be:

> You are the devil's gateway... [Y]ou are she who persuaded him who the devil did not dare attack... Do you not know that every one of you is an Eve? The sentence of God on your sex lives on in this age; the guilt, of necessity, lives on too.[9]

And, hence, we have the doctrine that women are created inferior, secondary, weak, and prone to evil, and that the first woman ruined everything for the perfect man. According to Tertullian, female shame, guilt, and punishment must continue indefinitely. And, being a very influential man, this idea settled deeply into Christian belief and the general culture (since it was indeed the general culture under Rome for a long time).

Today in the United States, the average woman makes 77 cents for each dollar earned by the average man holding the same level of education and same level of job responsibilities; for African American women it is 64 cents, and for Latinas it is 54 cents. In 2013, only twenty-one Fortune 500 companies (4.2 percent) had female CEOs, and women fill just 16.9 percent of corporate board seats.[10] Women have 20 seats out of the 100 in Congress, yet make up 51 percent of the U.S. population. We have not yet had a female President; while many other countries—India, Israel, Argentina, Great Britain, Pakistan, France, Canada, and multiple countries in Africa, just to name a few—have had female Presidents and Prime Ministers. In this way, we are indeed a "Christian nation."

I do not hear Jesus the zealot, the Child of Humanity and includer of women, in Christian doctrine; but I detect a lot of Roman philosophy, which was the male-dominated realm of intellectual, political, and spiritual pursuit. The Patristic Era (Latin/Greek patér or father) ran from the end of the Apostolic Age or New Testament times (around 100 C.E.) until around the eighth century. This era of religious thought and political and social formation included such noted and quoted intellectuals as Ignatius of Antioch, Justin Martyr, Pope Clement I, Irenaeus of Lyons, Clement of Alexandria, Origen, Athanasius, Basil of Caesarea, Gregory of Nyssa, Jerome, Augustine of Hippo, and our old friend Tertullian.

The scriptures and religious rules being debated and formulated were guided by trends in popular philosophical thought. For instance, Gregory of Nyssa was married and from a wealthy family in Asia Minor in the fourth century. It is said he resented having to live up to the expectations of friends, family, wife, and children, and the obligation of social and political involvement that was common for the elite of the Roman Empire. Therefore, he wrote longingly about the merits of asceticism—the trend involving abstinence, austerity, and transcendence of the body, believed to help men achieve the highest spiritual and moral level. He fervently wished he could "raise his own life above the world" to live solely for God and himself alone.[11]

First a rhetorician, he later became bishop of Nyssa (a Roman town in Cappadocia in Turkey). He wrote in theological terms about the superiority of the ascetic philosophy. He was strongly influenced not only by his personal desire to escape his family responsibilities, but by the writings of Origen and Neoplatonism, which were grist for his mill. As it would happen, Gregory was also involved in developing the doctrine of the Trinity and the Nicene Creed. This popular affinity Gregory of Nyssa had for the goal of transcending the body and physical life was the "gospel" of Platonic and Stoic philosophers.[12] Plato considered Socrates, his own teacher, to be the only person who truly attained this level of virtue, but a swath of early Christians believed it was within the reach of every convert to the new religion. They established it as a primary principle of Christianity, leaving the Child of Humanity—whose goal was to make us better humans and get his hands dirty bringing a new realm of freedom, equality, and dignity to the earthly here and now—in the dust.

Paul's teachings about asceticism must have been like catnip for men like Gregory. In the first letter to the Corinthians, Paul acknowledges that marriage is not sin, but asserts to new Christians that abstinence and physical transcendence are best. Then, interestingly, the text turns to interpret the second version of the creation story in Genesis 2: "For man was not made from woman, but woman from man. Neither was man created for woman, but woman for man" (1 Corinthians 11:9, NIV).[13] [Genesis 1, the other creation story, alternately indicates man and woman were created at the same time and given the same status].

Generations of Paul's followers debated what all this meant. Elaine Pagels says there were some groups who thought only those who would "undo the sin of Adam and Eve" (assuming it was based in sexual temptation) by being celibate were truly adhering to and able to claim the Christian gospel. But as mentioned earlier, this whole enterprise of ascetic celibacy threatened patriarchy by freeing women from the controlled transaction of marriage. Because of this, other groups who represented and influenced a majority of the early churches vehemently rejected celibate asceticism. As discussed, dissenters wrote letters in Paul's name, including 1 Timothy, and used the tale of Adam and Eve to enforce traditional marriage and the "Godly family structure," as well as to "prove that women, being naturally gullible, are unfit for any role but raising children and keeping house."[14]

Anywhere Paul speaks of asceticism, you can be sure that contradictory words about the submissive place of women will follow. And, hence, the myths of creation and Eve in the garden of Eden were used to protect and preserve patriarchal society in the face of its questioning.[15] They are still used today, in ways both obvious and unspoken. The complexity of the formulation of Christian doctrine over the centuries could fill another book or two, but here is one last important example. Pagels ultimately points to the influential fourth-century theologian and bishop Augustine:

> If any of us could come to our own culture as a foreign anthro-pologist and observe traditional Christian attitudes toward sexu-ality and gender, and how we view "human nature" in relation to politics, philosophy, and psychology, we might well be astonished at attitudes we take for granted. Augustine, one of the greatest teachers of western Christianity, derived many of these attitudes from the story of Adam and Eve: that sexual desire is sinful; that infants are infected from the moment of conception with the disease of original sin; and that Adam's sin corrupted the whole of nature itself. Even those who think of Genesis as only literature, and those who are not Christian, live in a culture indelibly shaped by such interpretations as these.[16]

Augustine altered Christian doctrine on freedom, sexuality, sin and redemption for all future generations, says Pagels. Whereas generations of Jews and groups of early Christians had found the Adam and Eve story to be about humanity's complex freedom to discern and choose, Augustine recast it as a dark story of human bondage to sin. Also, where the Bible does not overtly sexualize the story of Adam and Eve eating from the tree—it only notes that they became aware and ashamed of their nakedness and covered up afterward—Augustine makes sexual desire and the act of sex a prime villain in the story, and in the resulting doctrine.

Augustine read Genesis 1—3 and came away with the idea that the free will of humans as a whole is always and absolutely corrupt, that no person is capable of restraint or mastery of selfish, sexual impulses. Therefore, all of humankind is intrinsically fallen. He believed that sexual desire and death were not natural occurrences, but that both were introduced as punishment. Eating from the one fabled forbidden tree of knowledge in the garden, in his estimation, caused sex and death; despite that those are needed things for all species. So, of course, he had to include animals, trees, fish, insects, oceans, and mountains. All of creation became fallen. The Gospel of Mary comes to mind, and Jesus' warning about making extraneous law that entraps us. These doctrines grow like tumors to indict and condemn every living thing, paralyzing our freedom and our ability to stretch and grow, to really know the truth about ourselves and respect our environment.

This is why it helps to understand that Augustine's unfortunate interpretation of the texts and the resulting damning doctrine can be linked to his confused contempt for his own youthful sex drive and his conflicted relations with females. He struggled mightily with lust and thought a lot about man's perceived inability to control the sexual organ. He writes of his youth in his *Confessions:*

> Clouds of muddy carnal concupiscence filled the air. The bubbling impulses of puberty befogged and obscured my heart so that it could not see the difference between love's serenity and lust's darkness. Confusion of the two things boiled within me. It seized hold of my youthful weakness sweeping me through the precipitous rocks of desire to submerge me in a whirlpool of vice.[17]

I assume the lack of complete anatomical and biological knowledge during the time Augustine lived—and the widespread dependence upon religious explanation—prevented him from approaching the situation rationally. There was no coming up with a doctrine to illuminate what to expect from hormones during puberty, how to put a healthy sexual drive into context and perspective, and how to either take care of oneself or discipline oneself in the light of conscience. No, his sad solution was to believe that the whole of creation, humanity, and everything about everyone was utterly depraved. Furthermore, in Augustine's mind, his biological condition was the fault of women.

Around the age of thirty, having not been able to settle down and having gotten a talking-to from his mother, who hoped he would become a Christian, Augustine became engaged to a ten-year-old girl. While he waited a couple years for her to come of age, he couldn't resist taking on at least one other sexual tryst. Eventually he converted to Catholicism and took on celibate asceticism. But he could never quite get over his obsession with sex and women. As such, he determines:

> And as in [a man's] soul there is one power which rules by directing, [and] another made subject that it might obey, so also for the man was corporeally made a woman, who, in the mind of

her rational understanding should also have a like nature, in the sex, however, of her body should be in like manner subject to the sex of her husband, as the appetite of action is subjected by reason of the mind, to conceive the skill of acting rightly. These things we behold, and they are severally good, and all very good.[18]

Translated into modern English, he thinks women should be subject to men in the same way man's impulses must be subdued by the reasoning ability of the mind. Women do not just cause impulses, women are impulses. Men are the reasonable mind that controls the impulses. Men were created to control women. (Wait, who was the one battling uncontrollable lust, again?) Women's bodies are an unwieldy problem, and must be subjected either to man's mind control, or his sexual appetite.

In other words, he surmises that the solution to mankind's pesky problem of uncontrollable sexual urges is the submission of women. I present to you a prime example of the genesis of the modern rape culture, steeped in religious mansplaining. Yet he is known as "Saint" Augustine, and his thoughts on God, life, and the human condition—though not all as disturbingly dangerous as this one—are still the foundation of traditional Christianity.

Pagels observes of Augustine's influence: "This cataclysmic transformation in Christian thought from an ideology of moral freedom to one of universal corruption...coincided with the evolution of the Christian movement from a persecuted sect to the religion of the [Roman] emperor himself."[19] The goals and ethos of the Roman Empire were threaded into the texts and doctrines. Pagels goes on to say:

Augustine read back into Paul's letters his own teaching of the moral impotence of the human will, along with his sexualized interpretation of sin. Augustine's theory of original sin not only proved politically expedient, since it persuaded many of his contemporaries that human beings universally need external government—which meant, in their case, both a Christian state and an imperially supported church—but also offered an analysis of human nature that became, for better and worse, the heritage of all subsequent generations of western Christians and the major influence on their psychological and political thinking.[20]

Greco-Roman civilization was the primary influence at the foundation of today's Western civilization, including American universities, governing philosophies, economic systems, and Christian religious institutions. When we boil it down, the Augustine phenomenon is what feminists are still fighting: the corrupt lie that women were designed by God for men, and that we should be both controlled and exploited. Women of faith must understand these origins to create strategies that get back to the root of misogyny and sexism. This way, we can safely bring forward the more life-affirming ancient mythology to inform and create a new reality.

Society's Spin on Original Sin

In 1883, Lillie Devereux Blake (1833–1913), an American suffragist and reformer, wrote in *Woman's Place To-day*: "Every denial of education, every refusal of advantages to women, may be traced to this dogma [of original sin], which first began to spread its baleful influence with the rise of the power of the priesthood and the corruption of the early Church."[21] Doctrine affects how we view reality and classify or identify people. It also affects whether we identify *with* people or not. In this case, it trains men and women alike to withhold empathy from Eve.

Internationally renowned author and economist Jeremy Rifkin says in his book *The Empathic Civilization: The Race to Global Consciousness in a World in Crisis* that the "disconnect between our vision for the world and our ability to realize that vision lies in the current state of human consciousness."[22] By taking us on an epic tour of human history that leads to today's most serious issues—violence, climate change, economic upheaval, the widening gap between rich and poor—he shows that developing and practicing empathy is the key to our survival. Studying our trajectory of progress and setbacks over the centuries shows that our sporadic process of moving away from tribalism and defensive demonizing, and toward unity and compassionate connections, is what has kept us alive and allowed us to thrive.

Rifkin builds a brilliant argument that the emergence of a consistent empathetic human consciousness, with a strong capability to identify with others who are different from us, is the only thing that will ultimately save us. Unfortunately, we often teach children the opposite doctrine; we espouse and model reactions of fearful oppression, demoralization, and division in our political, economic, and religious spheres. Whether it is disdain for foreigners, immigrants, certain races, cultures, religions, LGBTQ people, or the female gender, the refusal to treat them the way we want to be treated ultimately will destroy us all.

Women's voices have been left out of the Bible, and also the mainstream history books. And I don't mean a few chapters about suffrage or major milestones—I mean our actual voices relaying our experiences and providing our assessments of events in human history. History is told from the perspective of powerful men whose views were recorded as fact.

This skews how we learn our own history and develop our worldview. Furthermore, women are represented in media in very limited iterations. The stories or images of intelligent, productive, justice-oriented, hard-working female leaders are not the ones that easily go viral or rake in the big bucks. So, how are men to connect more deeply with the reality of women as diverse, whole, and accomplished human beings? Sadly, women have a hard time connecting with the deeper, holistic reality about ourselves, too. It is tough to be what you cannot see.

The Representation Project produced the documentary film *Miss Representation* to expose "the media's limited and often disparaging portrayals of women and girls, which make it difficult for women to achieve leadership positions and for the average woman to feel powerful herself." I recommend watching the trailer now at film.missrepresentation.org. (I'll wait.) The website says: "In a society where media is the most persuasive force shaping cultural norms, the collective message that our young women and men overwhelmingly receive is that a woman's value and power lie in her youth, beauty, and sexuality, and not in her capacity as a leader."[23] The film reveals shocking statistics: Between 1937 and 2005 there were only thirteen female protagonists in animated films, and all but one had the primary aspiration of attracting male romantic interest. In 2011, only 11 percent of protagonists across all film genres were female; they were primarily looking for romance, too. Progress is slow, but *Zero Dark Thirty*, directed by Kathryn Bigelow, has the strongest, non-sexualized female lead character to date in a major box office film, and it was all over the 2012 Oscars, so there is hope.

Youth, beauty, and sexuality are all the things Augustine and our society have long imagined as the circumscribed yet devastating power of Eve. The only power she is willingly given also draws accusations that she asks for whatever abuse she receives. Those traits were simultaneously the allure and the fear, the demand and the excuse. It is the premise upon which we have sold movies, music, novels, video games, adult entertainment, and pornography…and also religion.

As subtly and nonchalantly as this is played out, it has monumental repercussions. Sue Monk Kidd says in *Dance of the Dissident Daughter:* "To understand why the Eden story is so important, we have to remember the extraordinary way origin myths operate in our psyches. In a way, humans are not made of skin and bones as much as we are made of stories. The Eden myth perhaps more than any other floats in our cells, informing our vision of ourselves and the world."[24] Case in point, we have witnessed a resurgence of legislators who keep the conviction of Eve up their sleeves.

Each time we make progress on policies that give women control over our own personhood and decisions, they pull out the old religious language that spurs automatic mistrust of women's experience, judgment, and virtue.

Candidates and Congresspeople mansplain family planning to us, and threaten our access to healthcare. They promise to repeal Roe vs. Wade, even for women who need abortions after incest or rape, and they show little to no interest in protecting the life of the mother when at risk. They believe the male-dominant government should control our decisions and our bodies, rather than letting us determine the best healthcare for ourselves with our doctors, families, and spiritual advisors. Politicians threaten to shut down Planned Parenthood, which provides life-saving medical care—including mammograms and pap smears—to low-income (and often middle-class) girls and women. We need leaders who see women as fully capable decision-makers for our own welfare and futures. Even if you do not believe abortion is a moral procedure—honestly, everyone believes it is the most heinous thing to have to decide and go through—the moral, emotional, and physical choice should belong to women in charge of our own bodies; as opposed to a dictatorship of men in government. Abortions are often an economic decision also supported by the man involved, but we do not shame the man. Sixty-one percent of abortions are performed on women who have one or more children already, and demand for abortions by married couples is rising.[25] And abortion is just one element of women's overall health and well-being. Did you know the U.S. ranks sixtieth of 180 countries studied for maternal mortality [death related to childbirth]? Our politicians don't talk about that. China, by contrast, is doing better, ranked at fifty-seventh.[26] But the patriarchy will only focus on what gives it the greatest justification for control.

During the 2012 election cycle, politicians put the moral burden on women to take the blame and even atone for violent crimes perpetrated against us by men. In their rhetoric, responsibility falls on the victim of rape and domestic abuse to somehow right the wrong done to her; to bear not just the pain and shame, but the economic burden of the consequences. Their response to women who are victims of domestic violence (1 in 4) or sexual assault (1 in 5) is not to talk about prevention measures, or how they will prosecute and punish offenders to bring justice and safety to women. Rather, these politicians respond with threats of outrageous insurance costs and blocks to access for needed mental and physical healthcare, and continue to delegitimize and stigmatize victims.

I hear a lot of rhetoric about how to regulate women's bodies and punish us for crimes committed against us. But I have never heard politicians suggest policies for stopping rape and domestic violence, regulating the bodies or autonomy of men, or punishing and humiliating them. That is, until President Obama's 2014 press conference on the launch of his new White House Task Force to Protect Students from Sexual Assault. He looked into the camera and said: "I want every young man in America to feel some strong peer pressure in terms of how they are supposed to behave and treat women."[27] In this day and age, the leader of the free world is forced to plead with society to respect girls and women in the face of an epidemic of campus sexual assault and lack of response by university authorities and police. Two-thirds of rapes are committed by someone known to the victim,[28] yet 68 percent of the assaults are not reported— because of the victims' fear of retribution, victim-blaming, getting fired from a job, or being ostracized and distracted at school. The majority of perpetrators are never questioned or investigated, much less prosecuted or convicted. Ninety-eight percent of rapists will never spend a day in jail.[29]

Women deserve to live in a safe and respectful environment. And we simply must have equal pay for equal work, equal representation in government, resources and support in the workplace, access to quality contraception, and affordable preventative and reproductive health services. Catalyst studies show that when women have equal employment opportunities, wages, and social support, it powerfully benefits families, businesses, communities, and societies.[30] When women are educated, paid well, and have meaningful, stable work, the result is that families, economies, and communities thrive. Family planning—the control over our own bodies and when, whether, and with whom we get pregnant—helps ensure this success by timing and spacing children when resources are secure. Access to affordable or free contraception in the U.S. by Title IX-funded clinics was shown in 2008 alone to avert 973,000 unintended pregnancies that would have statistically resulted in 406,000 abortions.[31] This is not just a "women's issue," it is a human rights issue and a global economic issue; it requires the attention of the men who are in relationships with women and are equally responsible for creating pregnancies and raising families.

If we will envision and respond to a new way, it will bring a better reality for all of us. Our most intractable dilemmas stem from the entrenched doctrine that male-dominant religion and government are ordained to run and regulate the very person—body, mind, and spirit—of women. Only a society that treats women as valuable, trustworthy, productive, and competent human beings made equal and in the image of God will ever rise to solve its most profound problems.

Who Are We, Really?

Not long ago I came across a website for a graphic design and production company called "Depraved Wretch." Its logo is black with a menacing font. It's tagline is "Exposing Human Nature, Extolling God's Mercy." Images on the home page include close-ups of people smiling too forcefully, and exuberant families running through gardens of flowers hand in hand. They advertise a T-shirt they designed featuring a shattered red heart that declares "God loves the unloveable." Their photography division does engagement photos.

In the section of the site called "What's with the name?" the company proudly states that most people don't understand the "true nature of mankind," and they are going to teach us all how terrible we are by spreading awareness via their business. "We believe that all of humanity is totally depraved, lost, blind and dead in sin," they say. "Every one of us deserves the wrath of God for every sin we've committed, but Jesus Christ took all of our sin upon Himself and suffered in our place. Turn from sin and put your faith and trust in Christ alone for salvation."[32] Then they give you a link to "get your very own Depraved Wretch wallpaper for your Desktop or iPhone." This is a common fundamentalist Christian worldview in which many of us were raised.

Unlovable, depraved, lost, sinful, wretched, worthless… What does this teaching do to us over time? It not only damages us psychologically, but also creates a relationship to God and others that is paralyzed with constant guilt and shame. A relationship that cannot move beyond the parent-child, reward-punishment formula. A relationship that cannot truly grow. When people are full of self-doubt and loathing, we either buy into whatever authorities say will save us, or we cower in disgust and fear in the corner, letting the undeserving world go to hell in a hand basket. And that gets us nowhere.

Most of us care about others and want the same things: peace, prosperity, love, a place to belong, and a contribution to make. There are indeed people who carry out atrocious acts; these actions stem from not only illnesses and backward teachings or influences, but frustration and anger generated when people are not given equal access or fair chances at fulfilling their basic human needs. This is one reason Jesus fought for a new reality. He stood up for those whom society labeled depraved because of their circumstances or differences.

No person, action, intention, idea, or invention is all good or all bad. For instance, the Internet puts the world at our fingertips: disseminating critical information, providing access to education, and facilitating connections. It also harbors child pornography and supports a social media network that has caused bullied people to commit suicide. Its character depends on how it is used by people. People do a spectrum of terrible things, and they must be held accountable and punished. But, interestingly, someone usually knows another side of them. For example, an older, retired police officer shoots a young father to death in a movie theater for texting his babysitter during the previews, but the murderer's children swear he is a good man and wonderful dad.[33] Mixtures of social cues about entitlement and control, personal fear and self-loathing, herd mentalities, normalization of violence, and addictions and disorders can make otherwise decent people into monsters. But there is a reason we are always shocked, outraged, and perplexed by it: because people are normally intrinsically well-meaning and good-hearted.

Masses of Christians cannot continue to accept doctrine that contradicts our observations, knowledge, and experience, and call it "truth." This is important for girls and women, because we so often take the brunt of the consequences in a society that has bought into the idea of humanity as intrinsically bad. Depravity becomes an excuse to turn a blind eye to interpersonal and systemic violence, and an argument that women deserve it. But we cannot afford to wait for a savior who will come back and take care of it one undisclosed day. Especially when Jesus modeled another way.

We must believe that we are innately good in order to cultivate our goodness. Viable solutions arise when we can appeal to our higher natures with confidence that we can access and operate from that core—and that we will be safe, supported, and respected when we choose to do so. We can only see a way out when we are able to truly recognize what a holistic, fully functioning human being is like (and admit it exists—note I didn't say "perfect") and understand and address the complex social problems and illnesses that trigger abnormal behavior. The Child of Humanity came to make us whole, well, empowered, compassionate, human beings—here and now, when it counts.

Most importantly, we must teach little girls that they are not sinful, evil, or dirty. Women do not deserve to be raped, punched, harassed, or called names; and, despite what anyone says, we do not play any role in criminal acts committed against us.[34] Our natural sexuality is positive and healthy—and it belongs to us; it is not something men own, not something "Jesus" or religion owns, not something for which we should be shamed, punished or exploited. We are not fallen; in fact, we are every moment taking our first steps without feet, soaring toward a secret sky. We are half the population, and we are the hope for a better world. No matter what they call us, our futures depend on knowing who we really are.

What's in a Name?

Elaine Pagels notes that many early Christians assumed that certain things are always good and others pure evil, and they intensely debated which belonged to which category. The Gospel of Philip, another text found with the hidden scriptures and Gnostic texts at Nag Hammadi, is a spiritual tool that can support our feminist faith by challenging the foundational way the moral questions that doctrine tries to answer and code into belief are set up. Pagels notes that in this text "the moral significance of any act depends upon the situation, intentions, and level of consciousness of the participants. This author of the Gospel of Philip characterizes such terms as 'good' and 'bad,' like other pairs of opposites, as merely mental categories."[35] The Gospel of Philip says:

> Light and darkness, life and death, right and left, are brothers of one another. They are inseparable. Because of this, the "good" are not good, nor the "evil" evil, nor is "life" life, nor is "death" death... The names given to things in the world are very deceptive (53:14–19, 24).[36]

Light and dark, life and death, right and left, yin and yang. Without one aspect of reality we do not have the other; both exist and are morally neutral. The author of Philip traces this deception of naming and dichotomizing back to the myth of the garden of Eden. Adam and Eve sought knowledge in the first first-known assertion of strict black and white categories: the mythical tree of the knowledge of good and evil. Religious doctrine was developed based on those same categories, which maintained this initial deception. "The law was the tree..." says the Gospel of Philip. "For when [the rulers, the law] said, 'Eat this, do not eat that,' it became the beginning of death" (74:5–12).[37] The restriction and polarization of knowledge into labels of good and evil—not the pursuit of knowledge itself—was the sin that brought death.

The Gospel of Philip flips the script on the whole enterprise by pointing out that a tree bearing fruit holding the knowledge of good and evil is a construction of deception in the first place. In the Gospel of Mary, Jesus warned against making doctrine that would trap us in a paradox that would prevent us from doing the right thing in different or unforeseen situations. Rather than getting us to heaven, these doctrines would create hell on earth for many vulnerable people. "Names given to the worldly are very deceptive, for they divert our thoughts from what is correct to what is incorrect," says the Gospel of Philip. We have been trained so that when we hear a term, we automatically assume something about its character, and we are often disillusioned or just plain wrong. This has real impact on how we think and act as women. The text goes on to say:

> Thus one who hears the word "God" does not perceive what is correct, but perceives what is incorrect. So also with "the Father" and "the Son" and "the Holy Spirit" and "life" and "light" and "resurrection" and "the Church (Ekklesia)" and all the rest—people do not perceive what is correct but they perceive what is incorrect, unless they have come to know what is correct. The names which are heard in the world...deceive. If they were in the Aeon (eternal realm), they would at no time be used as names in the world...
>
> But truth brought names into existence in the world for our sakes, because it is not possible to learn it (truth) without these names. Truth is one single thing; [yet] it is [presented as] many things and for our sakes to teach about this one thing in love through many things. The rulers [Greek *archons*; rulers, lords, or title of public office] wanted to deceive man... They took the name of those that are good and gave it to those that are not good, so that through the names they might deceive him and bind them to those that are not good...for they wanted to take the free man and make him a slave to them forever.[38]

No wonder the Gospel of Philip was not included by the *archons* themselves who canonized the New Testament! The God we are taught is not necessarily God. The institutional church that doles out doctrine is not exactly what it purports to be. As many of us have suspected, nothing is as it seems, and we have been convinced—maybe even threatened—to go along with the institution's naming of reality that this text claims was for the purpose of deception. As women, this resonates. We weren't allow to be involved in the creating and naming, and those early women who tried had their eyes scratched out, so we don't really know for sure what is actually behind the concepts: Father, Son, Holy Spirit, Church, light, life, resurrection. Why do words that sound good often belie so much evil? We've used these words with devotion all our lives, but do we truly know them and what they really represent?

Something the author of Philip says about the deceptive uses of names catches my imagination: *"people do not perceive what is correct, but they perceive what is incorrect, unless they have come to know what is correct."* This sense of "coming to know the correct" points to lessons learned by our female experience. We cannot be told by men in power what is correct; we must come to know it ourselves. It points to our deep inner knowledge of what makes sense when we listen to the voice of God, revealing to us that what is often said about us and done to us is wrong. How else would we simply "come to know what is correct" after being deeply inculcated into imperial doctrine that suppresses women and elevates men? We sense that anything less than the freedom, authenticity, and wholeness of women is not right; but it takes a lot of trial and error for many of us to truly learn and know that.

It can be hard to imagine letting go of the religious dichotomy of good and evil and living more confidently in the real nuances of our experiences. It leaves a void where stories, people, and events had been strictly defined, moralized, and polarized for us. Resisting the predefined means we have to hang in the balance, doing a lot of scary, lonely work questioning the status quo and peeling back the layers of our religion and society and everything we've constructed our lives upon. But the void created, the Gospel of Philip hints, is where everything we really need actually is. This presupposes being able to separate the reality of God from human doctrine. It involves doubting—not necessarily God's existence—but how God has been falsely characterized and limited, how we as human beings and as women have been falsely characterized and limited by doctrine. As theologian Paul Tillich said in *The Courage to Be*:

> The courage to take the anxiety of meaninglessness upon oneself is the boundary line up to which the courage to be can go. Beyond it is mere non-being. Within it all forms of courage are re-established in the power of the God above the God of theism. The courage to be is rooted in the God who appears when God has disappeared in the anxiety of doubt.[39]

There is a God who shows up when we let all the false gods, the indoctrinated gods, go. As feminists of faith, we must be willing to go to the place of the unknown and the ostracized, where we can meet the God of freedom and equality. Many traditional Christians will not like it, and you will know how threatened they are by how indignant or angry they get. In *A New Evangelical Manifesto: A Kingdom Vision for the Common Good*, theologian Brian McLaren says:

> Just as the Christian faith was deeply embedded in Medieval culture to such a degree that modern expressions of the Christian faith were considered heretical, so today Christian faith is deeply embedded in modern culture to such a degree that post-modern

explorations are considered heretical. Just as the emergence of Christian faith from its Medieval context was gradual and diverse, so the current emergence of Christian faith will take time to develop and will take many forms.[40]

So, as long as we are the inventors of modern, autonomous, single womanhood, why not also create a doctrine of coming to know what is correct? For now, the only requirement is un-learning and un-believing everything we have been taught, like Rumi suggested in our earlier meditation. Christopher Morse would suggest to us the option of engaging what he calls "faithful disbelief" along the lines of the tradition of John, which says: "Beloved, do not believe every spirit, but test the spirits to see whether they are from God; for many false prophets have gone out into the world" (1 John 4:1, NRSV). We hear the familiar buzz of false prophets every day. We are to test the spirit of texts, doctrines, language, actions, images and beliefs to see if there is equality, autonomy, freedom, and respect. Look for release from captivity, the recovery of sight, the year of the jubilee that Jesus set in motion. That is where God is present.

As Morse says, "To believe in God is at once to disbelieve what is not of God. Faith in God, we are led to conclude, is not only believing; it is disbelieving as well."[41] The doctrine of disbelief is where we can start to rebuild. We call out what we disbelieve in this world, and preach and teach it to the generations; that is feminism. Our hearts and intuition already know what we truly want to become; that is faith. And we follow the way of Jesus because we have a new reality to create.

DEVOTIONAL: What Eve Knows

In some Gnostic texts, Eve is the representative of spiritual principle and higher awareness, a subversive and offensive idea in patriarchal times. Eve is a primal spiritual intelligence who emerges inside Adam as soul or spiritual awareness, and awakens him. The stories recount how Eve is later met with resistance by society, and is "misunderstood, attacked, and mistaken for what she [is] not."[42] The authors of these texts were already seeing women being oppressed, and were speaking out. They were quickly silenced.

The Gnostic text *Reality of the Rulers* portrays Adam, upon first seeing Eve, as recognizing her as a spiritual power in her own right.

And when he saw her, he said, "It is you who have given me life: you shall be called Mother of the Living [Eve]; for it is she who is my Mother. It is she who is the Physician, and the Woman, and She Who Has Given Birth.[43]

Here, the creators mentioned in Genesis 1:26; 3:22; and 11:7 (i.e., "let us make the human in *our* image") are considered to be the *archons* or rulers, not a cosmic God. The main *archon* in *Reality of the Rulers*, who is so concerned with regular people gaining the knowledge of good and evil, is named Samael, or "god of the blind." The story says, "[H]is thoughts became blind." The nefarious rulers warn Adam not to listen to Eve, and he loses contact with her spirit. Later, she reappears to him in the garden in the form of a serpent. The snake in Rulers is not evil, as portrayed in Genesis; rather, it manifests the Female Spiritual Principle, acknowledged by many spiritual groups still today. Eve the serpent asks the man and the "woman of flesh" in the garden (in this story, that character is separate from Eve) if it is true that the archon told them not to eat from the tree. The woman of flesh says that yes, he said they would die if they ate of it. The "Snake, the Instructor" (Eve) responds that they will not die, but that their eyes shall be opened, and they will be sighted with knowledge. Maybe this is another reason why women were excluded and oppressed when Christianity became formalized under the empire; because at one point Eve was known as something entirely different than a slut who screwed up and ruined everything. She was a being of knowledge, wisdom, and discernment that slid around the false barriers of power and empowered everyone equally, making regular humans smart and savvy enough to challenge the deceptive gods who ruled the world.

Likewise, Jesus, in his announcement of his good news or gospel, says God sent him to restore sight to the blind. Blindness has a special meaning; it was the primary ailment Jesus addressed. Sight, or knowledge, is key to the salvation and redemption of humanity: freedom, equality, dignity, opportunity to reach our potential. Restoration indicates that sight is something we possessed naturally, but lost because of some larger deception, which the Gospel of Philip hints at as being the initial imperial religious institution and its doctrinal naming. You may recall instances when Jesus would heal the blind and then instruct them not to tell anyone, especially the religious leaders. He did not want those religious leaders to catch on, until it was too late, to the fact that so many eyes were being opened. This would incite the rulers to take further oppressive action, because regular people would be able to detect and rise up against their deception. Many of Jesus' stunts were attempts to get people to see the corruption of the rulers, to truly discern our inherited naming of things and our imbedded assumptions about them. He called out the religious leaders who deceptively named what was good as bad, and bad as good. We can do this, too.

In contrast to Jesus, the representation of God in the biblical Eden story was deeply concerned about the possibility of the first humans' eyes being opened: our ability to see and know the difference between good and evil, to gain knowledge, to become like the ruling gods. If we do not know the difference, we will blindly follow the principles of those who assert or abuse power, those who manipulate us to make their rules seem all good. To keep humans from having knowledge, the Genesis version of God hung death over their heads—a concept the man and woman supposedly would not have known yet, and would not have been able to judge as a good or bad thing. Being told knowledge will lead to our death is quite an intimidating tactic.

The *archons* tried to control and suppress humans by convincing them good was bad, and knowledge was deadly. Eve in *Reality of the Rulers* rationally points out that the opposite is actually the case—knowledge is like sight given to the blind. It equips us with insight, awareness, discernment, foresight, intelligence, and choice—choices for a better life, not certain death. It indeed gives us power. Knowledge promotes intentional integration of the body, mind, soul, and spirit; of ourselves and others. It makes us whole. Knowledge opens our eyes to new realities; it is the only way to bring a new world—the realm of God—into being.

Reflection:

- What has the symbol of the tree of the knowledge of good and evil meant in your upbringing, faith tradition, and life as a woman?
- In what ways have you been taught that bad is good, or good is bad? How has this affected your life?
- How does it change your feelings about the Eden story and its doctrine, to flip the script and see Eve placed in a powerful, high-minded, heroic position?
- What kind of goals for the integration of spirituality and knowledge might you make for yourself in light of this new vision of Eve?

CHAPTER 5

The Pinnacle of Womanhood

Give to the women of our time the strength to persevere, the courage to speak out, the faith to believe in [God] beyond all systems and institutions....
—SISTER JOAN CHITTISTER

The most common way people give up their power is by thinking they don't have any. — ALICE WALKER

My friend Lourds Lane is a rock star. Literally. An Indie sensation and front for the rock band LOURDS, she is also the creator and writer of the book, music, and lyrics for an upcoming Broadway musical and global girls' empowerment movement called *Chix 6*. The story centers on six female superheroines who represent different aspects of the authentic power girls hold inside. Lourds began training on violin and piano at age three, played Carnegie Hall at six, and toured with orchestras around the world throughout her youth. She graduated from Harvard with honors in English and American literature, the youngest in her class. She also created the Medusa Festival, an annual event featuring the best emerging female-fronted bands in the U.S.

Lourds is a ball of energy, wit, and vision. She cares deeply about people and justice in the world. She knows herself and her own story well, and she moves intentionally at full force to fulfill her purpose by doing what she loves. Born and raised Catholic in Jamaica, Queens, New York, she was not the kind who tucked herself neatly into the hierarchy of the church; but she did give her childhood tradition another shot later on. Recently, she told me the story:

It was my first trip to Rome. Holy Moly See. It was a big deal. I am a Filipino-American and my Filipino peeps populate the third-largest Catholic country in the world. My mom grew up in the Philippines and was the proud president of the Catholic Student

107

Association of St. Teresa's in St. Marcelino. She raised her
children to be devout Catholics and I followed all the church rules
like a good Catholic school girl until 6th grade. Then came my
rebellious, truth-seeking teen years. I traded my classical acoustic
violin for an electric violin that could distort like a guitar. I started
my own rock band. The first day I experienced the "gift" of music
and lyrics shooting out of me like starlight, I dropped to my knees
and cried.

I learned that I could pull out music in silence. Suddenly, I
discovered a deeper connection to the divine in the act of writing
music than listening to the sermons at church. I say "listened" very
loosely because my hour and a half of obligatory church time
became equivalent to afternoon nap time. I became the master
of the steady, slightly cocked neck position where my closed eyes
could possibly look like I was deep in contemplation. During this
time, my mother was sleepless, working long hours as a single
mom. She was ecstatic that I was the top of my class academically.
So despite my rock band, I was enough of a goodie two shoes to
bend the rules. Church wasn't for me so I just stopped going.

Back to Holy Moly. It was a special event in Rome. For the
low, low price of 3–5 hours in line, you could confess your sins
to an ARCHBISHOP. Wow! What are the chances? I took it as
a sign. I am here for a reason, I thought. This is an opening, a
chance to get guided back to my faith! After 20 years, I've come
back home in Rome! I was nervous while waiting in line. I wasn't
sure I remembered the rules. How do I do this again? Do I get on
my knees from the beginning? Sign of the cross? A prayer? Then
what do I say? The TRUTH?

After 20 years, many of them traveling in a van with a rock
band, my "sins" might be a tad juicier than coveting Mary Elena's
juju-bees at lunch. But really, nothing THAT bad. I'm a good
person. These Archbishops must hear everything. I could talk
about one drunken moment and just be authentic. As a matter of
fact, I SHOULD do that. Just be full out me. Excited and WIDE
AWAKE at church! Yes, this could be my awakening!

To ease my nerves, I decided I would channel the divine
connection I feel when I write to music. It will all be natural. I
will think of the juiciest and sinniest moment and share openly
and freely. God will be in the confessional. I will be received with
acceptance and love. In my three hours of waiting in line, I saw

the whole thing play out. In the end of our time together, Archie would welcome me home and maybe pass me a juju-bee through the little door. The Catholic Church and me would be BFFs again. "I'll see you next Sunday, my old friend." The image was clear. I couldn't wait to share.

I got to the front of the line and the "sin" I decided to share lingered on the tip of my tongue. I had practiced saying it in my head for three hours so I got the story down to 20 words. I'm polite. The line is so oppressively long so blabbing was not an option. Yep, few words but it's a doozy. I stepped inside the little room. I knelt. The little door opened and it was like riding a bike. "Forgive me father for I have sinned, it's been 20 years since my last confession..." I took a deep breath and prepared to launch into my 20 word sin. He didn't let me start. "You are Catholic and you have not come to church in 20 years?" he asked. "Well, yes," I said.

"Why have you not come to church in 20 years?" My palms got sweaty. I'm a grown woman and I knew I was in big trouble. "Well, it's not like I stopped believing in God. I pray all the time. I just don't go to church. I have a personal relationship with God." He wasn't having it.

"You are a Catholic and as a Catholic, it's a mortal sin to not go to church!" He then proceeded to tell me how often I should be attending church, how often I need to confess, how often I should tithe, how I will need to say 52,000 Hail Marys and Our Fathers and a prayer that I forgot how to say. Well, maybe not that many prayers...but I had tuned him out by then.

I felt ripped off. That's not my sin! I waited three hours and I didn't get to share the sin I wanted to share! I thought there might be a window in the end when I could squeeze in my 20 words real quick. But no such luck. He reprimanded me for about three minutes, rattling off the "rules" of the Catholic Church like an auctioneer, and then I felt the proverbial "boot" out of the confessional. I didn't get my juju-bee and I haven't been to confession since.

It is extremely disheartening when we squish ourselves up to fit into our little place in the religious hierarchy, to meet it on its terms, and there is not one juju-bee to be found. In the confessional was just an ordinary man. The man claiming to be her authorized intermediary to God left Lourds feeling devalued and disconnected. In his eyes she was doing nothing right, even though he knew absolutely nothing about her. And his position of power over her was dedicated to admonishing and punishing her, making the rules bigger than her humanity, seeing her—and trying his best to get her to see herself—as insufficient and unworthy.

But God fills her with music and starlight, creates with her, brings her to her knees with tears of pure joy and awe. God was no doubt there that day in Rome. But God was waiting outside in line with her for hours thinking about what her faith meant to her in the context of her life's journey. God was with her as she mused about where her spiritual seeking will take her next. God was there in her hope to reconnect with her tradition, and there when it was dashed. Our communion with God is not dependent upon the hierarchy, no matter how much they want us to believe it is.

Clergy are ordained into service to provide sustenance and guide individuals and communities along a path of symbols, images, and language that points to God. Clergy are not God and should not be playing God. How does the idea of the confessional intermediary between the authoritarian pinnacle of the church and the lowest on the totem pole work in the age of self-actualization and the spread of democracy? Does it create strong people of faith, or lost sheep dependent on someone else to appease God?

This is not confined to the Catholic Church. You can hear the hierarchy in Protestant God-talk, and, hence, traditional Protestant sensibilities. Strains of the state ring in military and feudal titles such as "Sovereign Lord," "Ruler of the Heavens and Earth," "the Almighty King on His Throne." Jesus counter-utilized the hierarchical language of the occupying Roman Empire to empower his movement of "the least of these." Hundreds of years passed and, as Roman elite were imbued with the power to create Christendom, such terms were used to undergird an earthly monarchy and a church-sanctioned caste system in its misleading interpretation of Jesus' "kingdom" of God. Some interpret the spread of Christianity as the miraculous hand of God working through men and history to raise up the "right" religion into world dominance. But that was not what Jesus was after.

Constantine was the son of a successful military general and a revered general himself. He and his co-emperor Licinius, who controlled the Balkans under Rome, collaborated to issue the Edict of Milan in 313, which legally tolerated Christianity. Not long after came the Battle of Chrysopolis, a power-grab between the emperors. As the victor, Constantine had Licinius unceremoniously executed. That's the kind of Lord he was and the kind of kingdom he ran. After Roman authorities had exterminated outspoken early Christians like pests for decades, it is said that Constantine had a mysterious vision. A local bishop interpreted the vision in his own way, making an allusion to the governing paradigm of Israel's King David. The emperor ended up converting to Christianity not so much out of spiritual conviction, but out of his interest in replicating this model of power.[1]

Constantine became a patron of the religion, but sanctioned only churches that had combined the Old Testament with their Christian literature that would become known as the New Testament. He chose the group that kept using the Old Testament (which other early churches had criticized for holding on to Jewish traditions of Israel) in order to highlight the kings of Israel and reverence for King David. By doing so, he established and acted out the heady relationship presented in the Old Testament between government and piety, rulership and religion, royalty and righteousness. Richly robed in this vision of himself, he began to target and persecute those Christians who did not use the Old Testament or Hebrew Bible as part of their scriptures. He went after the Gnostics with a vengeance.[2]

There followed a great purging of the diversity of early Christians, replaced with strict orders to establish orthodoxy and single-minded Christian teaching. The emperor rebuilt Jerusalem—which his predecessors had decimated—with majestic Christian basilicas. He took on the role of "imperial artistic director" in his quest to emulate the grandeur and religious power of David and Solomon.[3] Along the way, he went about conquering the people and lands around him from East to West and indoctrinating them into his Christendom.

According to Professor Shaye J.D. Cohen, Harvard University Professor of Hebrew Literature and Philosophy, Constantine operated in "this amazing position of having a theology of government that he [could] use to consolidate his own secular power." But it worked both ways. "The bishops now basically [had] federal funding to have sponsored committee meetings so they [could] try to iron out creeds and get everybody to sign up."[4] Cohen continues:

> The bishops are terribly grateful for this kind of imperial attention... The lines of power are unambiguous. Constantine is absolutely the source of authority. And there's no question about that. But the bishops are able to take advantage of Constantine's mood and his curious intellectual interest in things like Christology and the Trinity and Church organization. They're able to have Bibles copied at public expense. They are finally able to have public Christian architecture and big basilicas. So there's a comfortable

symbiotic relationship between the empire and the church, one that, in a sense, is what defines the cultural powerhouse of Europe and the West.[5]

A powerhouse that, centuries later, Europeans who would later become the first "Americans" fled in order to establish freedom of religion and autonomous personhood, with a crazy idea about government not by the hierarchal church, but for the people, by the people. A powerhouse that nonetheless still influences our culture today.

A succession of emperors came after Constantine, and an edict jointly issued by Theodosius I, Gratian, and Valentinian II made Christianity the state religion of Rome in 380. Pope Damasus I was influential in the proceedings; which legitimized a single expression of the faith across the empire, establishing it as catholic (meaning "universal") and orthodox (meaning "correct in teaching"). Theodosius went to great lengths to suppress all non-Nicene forms of Christianity. And the Nicene Creed, as we saw earlier, still affirms that rule today. Christian worship still uses images of bowing before thrones, lying prostrate in worship before the King, praising the majesty of the Lord. We plead for God's "benevolence," which originally referred to an indentured servant taken under contract of a master to work off his debt or escape enslavement. It fits the traditional narrative of divine salvation. Christians sing about unworthy sinners and lowly subjects joining the vast army of the Almighty Lord, marching to victory, conquering the world, sitting in glory at the right hand of the throne, sharing in heavenly riches. It seems the Christian kingdom must always be pitted against an evil foe.

As generations evolve, the language of serf-like subservience no longer provides comfort or hope for many of us. If we are praying daily for the obedience to submit to a greater will, we will probably achieve it; but in ways we did not intend. This is especially true for girls, who learn we are second-class from a complex combination of social cues. We do not need more of that hierarchal manipulation from our faith practice.

The New Power

Author and activist Gloria Feldt asks: "What would the world be like if women held most of the positions of power and leadership?" In her book *No Excuses: Nine Ways Women Can Change How We Think About Power*, Feldt explores the boundary-laden, often skittish and ambivalent relationship women have to power. "Power, through most of human history, has been a concept rooted in brute force, the *power-over* something or someone," she observes. "Because women have usually been among those over whom the powerful rule, it's no wonder that when we think about power we imagine negatives."[6]

Feldt points out typical ways women avoid or give up power. We may hesitate to speak first, or apologize constantly in conversation. Most do not rush confidently to put ourselves out there, take risks, and get our ideas into the marketplace the way men do. We are often taught to hang back and let others get their piece of the pie first, or to respectfully give others the floor. We are made to feel rude, egotistic, selfish, bossy, or bitchy if we try to lead. Whereas men tend to believe anything they have to say is important, women are socialized to worry that what we think or say has no intrinsic value. Men are encouraged to confidently pursue their self-interests from boyhood, while we often struggle to push boundaries or even negotiate salaries and roles. We have been conditioned by a male-run society and family structure to perform this dynamic.

Feldt says our aversion stems from the long tradition of "power-over," and our terrible experiences of it. Power is not innately bad; like the Internet, it depends upon how it is used. At face value, power is simply the ability to do, the capability to act, the possession of strong authority and agency. But power has been hoarded and overlorded, and especially distorted by religious institutions and their false hierarchy of male over female, human over creation. This has led to disasters ranging from wars to economic crises to environmental distress.

Feldt calls on women to redefine power so that we can embrace it and enact it on new and better terms. She calls this "power-to" and names it "the next iteration of leadership." Power-to is collaborative and equality-driven, without diminishing leadership skills and unique gifts. It assumes that, together, we have the power to do anything. Instead of subduing people from the top-down, it fosters cooperation. "It takes skill to *lead* others rather than to force, require, coerce, or lord over them," Feldt says [emphasis mine].[7]

The practice of equal-opportunity leadership encourages people, regardless of gender or identity, to use our interests and talents at the highest levels of influence to solve problems, invent solutions, and create positive change. But hierarchy is not fond of change. Often those top-tier people who utilize power-over believe that when opportunities and improvements are made for more vulnerable people on the lower rungs, this threatens or takes away their top-tier rights. These "male rights" or "religious rights" are also known as the historical ability to enforce their gender-based authority to subject others to their opinions and decisions.

"Power-over makes people feel power*less*," Feldt points out. It forbids our God-given ability to do, our capability to act. She reminds us that the capacity to choose is what sets us apart and makes us human beings, and that choosing is the basis of morality. When people are manipulated or stripped of control over themselves, and not allowed to exercise that central faculty, they become "disgruntled, angry, or passive-aggressive."[8]

Power-to recognizes the innate value and power of the individual. Power-to wants to partner and harness those things for the good of the community. Power-to not only welcomes but cultivates and supports the strengths, ideas, and perspectives of diverse individuals. "Power-over is amoral," Feldt says, and, in my estimation, immoral too. But "power-to is responsibility," she says.[9] It is all of us taking equal responsibility for society in the unique ways in which we are qualified and impassioned. The Child of Humanity knew that self-realization makes us the best humans we can be.

"Nuns on the Bus" began a tour across several states in 2012 to highlight what Roman Catholic sisters do: work with the disenfranchised about whom Jesus spoke so passionately. They stopped at food pantries, homeless shelters, healthcare clinics, and schools run by nuns across the country to call attention to the gospel they live by. The nuns may be low on the hierarchical pole in terms of power and visibility, but they are a force that sustains many communities every day.

The bus tour was spearheaded after the Vatican's reprimand of American nuns was released by its doctrinal office: the Congregation for the Doctrine of the Faith. The report said that the Leadership Conference of Women Religious (LCWR), the largest membership organization for nuns and sisters in the United States, had "challenged church teaching on homosexuality and the male-only priesthood, and promoted 'radical feminist themes incompatible with the Catholic faith'," according to *The New York Times*.[10] The group was accused of making public statements that "disagree with or challenge the bishops, who are the church's authentic teachers of faith and morals," and of course, are all men. Unbeknownst to the sisters, the Vatican had begun investigating them in 2008.

Sister Simone Campbell discovered that Network, the Catholic social justice lobby run by sisters, of which she is the current executive director, was also cited in the same document for "focusing its work too much on poverty and economic injustice, while keeping 'silent' on abortion and same-sex marriage."[11] An archbishop was assigned along with a couple of bishop-assistants by the Vatican to do something about these nuns. The big-brother bishops were given five years to completely rewrite the group's statutes. They will replace the handbook the nuns use to facilitate discussion on issues the Vatican says are settled doctrine and should not be discussed. The overseers also must approve of every speaker LCWR and Network has at public events. What kind of set up is this, if not imperious power-over?

At the same time, the Vatican was also quietly conducting other investigations, politely known as "visitations," of all American women's orders and organized religious communities affiliated with the Roman Catholic Church. Hierarchy spends a great deal of time, effort, manpower, and money keeping its "lower half" in line. Yet ironically, at this point there is still no effort within the church to imprison (or even punish) priests and bishops who engage in the criminal activity of sexually abusing children. The harsh, controlling hand of canonical law is above the law—both its own and that of the states in which it operates around the world.

The nuns' bus tour coincided with the 2012 U.S. Presidential election cycle. One of the tours' protests was against the House of Representatives' proposal to cut funding to programs for working families and those at or below the poverty line: an initiative led by Paul Ryan, a self-professed Catholic. "We're doing this because these are life issues," Sister Campbell said. "And by lifting up the work of Catholic sisters, we will demonstrate the very programs and services that will be decimated by the House budget."[12] The sisters engaged power-to with "the least of these" against the power-over of those privileged few who legislate the lives and futures of the lower rungs.

Simultaneously, groups of bishops were touring the country complaining that giving federal recognition and equal rights to gay people was a direct attack on Catholic religious liberty. They had the same complaint about giving women access to birth control and related healthcare through the Affordable Care Act and insurance offered through religious employers. Religious institutions demand employees uphold their doctrine against contraception, even though an overwhelming 98 percent of Catholic women (and their partners) who are sexually active use birth control anyway.[13] Power-over is about the will of the rulers; power-to is about the real lives of people. On the bus trail, one group was riding for the freedom and release from oppression of those on the lower rungs, and the other was riding to ensure the rule of its own hierarchical power and doctrine.

The nuns were back out on the trail in 2013, this time with the bishops in agreed support of immigration reform and the ability of our country to welcome the stranger and love our neighbors. No amount of protest has stopped them. And there has been plenty from those who feel the nuns are misinterpreting their faith or have no business rallying to affect lawmaking.

These nuns are subverting the hierarchy that entraps them by taking to the streets and fertilizing the grass roots with hope and love.

Pope Francis has said the Roman Catholic Church should stop focusing so exclusively on its position against abortion and homosexuality, and start paying more attention to the plight of the poor and marginalized in the tradition of Jesus. But, unfortunately, he reaffirmed the ongoing investigation and review of LCWR and Network in 2013. Despite this, Sister Simone and the nuns have kept their focus on faith-based social justice. She has spoken out to raise the low federal minimum wage, which disproportionally affects single working moms, saying, "We have a chance now to renew our social contract and to make sure that hardworking Americans earn enough to support their families." Because of their faith (a different thing than religious tradition), no matter how ugly the fight against the sisters gets, they will never get off the proverbial bus. "This is part of my pro-life stance and the right thing to do," Sister Simone said.[14]

When I think of how far women of faith have come using their voices for social change despite opposition, I can't help but think about Sojourner Truth. Her father was captured from the Gold Coast in what is now Ghana. She was born into slavery in 1797 in Ulster County, New York, and at age nine, sold as a package with a flock of sheep for $100 to a cruel man named John Neely. She bravely escaped to freedom in 1826 with her baby daughter, and went on to contribute to the abolitionist and women's movements. Her extemporaneous "Ain't I a Woman?" speech at the 1851 Ohio Women's Rights Convention in Akron shows us how to subvert the hierarchy. Truth spoke poignantly to the chasm between the treatment of black women in comparison to white women, who were also fighting an uphill battle for rights, but without the tremendous weight of slavery. She exposed the phenomenon of men creating false dichotomies, flattering women with petty pedestals and meaningless poetic images in order to distract us from true equality:

> That man over there says that women need to be helped into carriages, and lifted over ditches, and to have the best place everywhere. Nobody ever helps me into carriages, or over mud-puddles, or gives me any best place! And ain't I a woman?[15]

She flips the shame of abuse and hard labor into pride in her strength and fortitude: "Look at me! Look at my arm! I have ploughed and planted, and gathered into barns, and no man could head me! And ain't I a woman?"[16] Who needs to be patronized with help over a silly mud puddle? Not a woman of wisdom, vitality, and resilience. She also gave a powerful critique of the Christian clerical hierarchy's view of women:

Then that little man in black there, he says women can't have as much rights as men, 'cause Christ wasn't a woman! Where did your Christ come from? Where did your Christ come from? From God and a woman! Man had nothing to do with him.[17]

She goes on to subvert the traditional myth of Eve: "If the first woman God ever made was strong enough to turn the world upside down all alone, these women together ought to be able to turn it back, and get it right side up again!"[18] She deftly played on the patriarchy's version of reality to show they are still wrong about women: we are wise and strong, and we use our power for good.

Leaning In or Giving In?

Like Sojourner Truth, women have been leaning in to outspoken leadership in society for centuries in our own unique ways, even from our position at the bottom of the ranks. We have worked with whatever level of education and the few resources available to flip the script, no matter how colossal its size and scope. We have told our stories in whatever pauses we could squeeze them. Sometimes we fail to look back and marvel over how brave, bold, intelligent, and creative women have been in order to get where we are today. It is a hard-won place achieved by working tirelessly against the grain.

Sheryl Sandberg is the Chief Operating Officer of Facebook and one of the few women in the highest ranks of executive leadership in the tech sector. Her astute business sense, high-level experience, and feminist vision converge into sage advice that encourages women to confidently pursue influential positions in corporate America, despite the undeniable gender biases and roadblocks we still consistently encounter. She says we just have to go in and put our hats in the ring for the big projects, and then tough it out through the trials until we get to a higher level that affords us some control over the work environment for ourselves and other women. She is right that taking career risks to gain power—despite feeling uncertain or under-qualified—creates positive ripples.

However, many women do not care to "lean in" to the corporate world; not because they are not ambitious and smart, but because they are repelled by the hierarchical systems of power-over in which they are forced to conform behaviorally and ideologically. I spent thirteen years in advertising and branding for Fortune 500 companies, and there were a lot of "walking zombies." No one should be forcing themselves to go through the motions in a toxic work environment to rise through the ranks simply because "we need more women up there." We do need them there, but we also have to be authentic and fulfilled for this endeavor to be successful. So if it isn't true to you, don't sell your soul. What we really need are more women living into their deeper meaning and purpose, making a difference by doing what they were born to do. The hierarchy will keep trying to convince us that we can work out our differences. Ann Marie Slaughter says in her review of Sandberg's *Lean In*:

> [G]iven [Sandberg's] positions first at Google and now at Facebook, it is hard not to notice that her narrative is what corporate America wants to hear. For both the women who have made it and the men who work with them, it is cheaper and more comfortable to believe that what they need to do is simply urge younger women to be more like them...rather than make major changes in the way their companies work.[19]

I would not convict Sandberg of collusion; she is speaking from her experience of shattering a major glass ceiling, and is doing a great service for women with her programs. However, it is important to question whether we should be pushing women to find success by behaving like, and aspiring to, the hierarchy, or if the hierarchical institutions should continue to be pushed to change and support new models of diverse leadership. The second scenario is obviously much more difficult to bring into reality. I have multiple female friends going through unwanted battles because they stood up to higher-ranking men who asked them to flirt with clients, spoke to them with demeaning language, or threatened their positions if they followed their consciences. It is a struggle to risk our livelihoods for what we believe. It is not a quota of women at desks or in corner offices doing things the way they have always been done that matters; it is genuine female leadership and power-to that will make the difference.

Fearless Faith

I cannot get Sandberg's question out of my head: *What would you do if you weren't afraid?*[20] There are probably a million answers across all aspects of our lives. *I would assert my opinion. I would follow my instincts. I would confront someone who speaks disrespectfully about women. I would apply for grad school. I would break up with the person who undermines my confidence. I would be myself in every situation.*

In the evangelical environment in which I grew up, women around me pretended, or perhaps actually believed, that everything was as it was meant to be, no matter how unhappy they were or how much they suffered. I heard only the patriarchy's booming voice, assuring me all was in order. When a girl cannot hear or see anything else, she cannot know anything better exists. Girls must be taught the history, vocabulary, and tools needed see and believe in another reality. I like the PBS resource *Makers: Women Who Make America*, a series of online stories, interviews, and documentaries that provide the first-ever comprehensive overview of the women's movement (pbs.org/makers). Simply telling girls "you can do anything" is not enough; they need to actually see how.

Girls needs dissidents to emulate, since supporting the patriarchy rewards females with a false feeling of superiority and safety, in exchange for believing we can be free and successful under the ultimate control of men.

But the hierarchy not only oppresses women, it damages all of society. Harvard theologian and feminist icon Elisabeth Schüssler Fiorenza coined the term *kyriarchy*, formed from the Greek *kyrios* (lord or master) and *archō* (to lead, govern, or rule), to point out that even though the male gender is privileged by societal structures, men too can be oppressed by elite males at the top of the hierarchy.

Whereas patriarchy denotes social organization in which the father or father figures are supreme authority in the family, community, and greater world, kyriarchy describes a broader socio-political set-up in which the male noblesse rule over males of lower rungs, in addition to the whole of the female gender. Rather than being based on gender alone, domination is fueled by elements such as wealth, education, power, class, race, and sexual orientation. Schüssler Fiorenza sees feminism as a movement to raise the consciousness of both females and males. It is meant to allow us all to see, interpret, and address the structures that we are entangled within that oppress, limit, and abuse us.

Galen Guengerich once said, "Religion in its traditional sense has made the world a very dangerous place for women, and it's horrific." But he also noted that wise people know that women being relegated to the bottom of the hierarchy is bad for men, women, and children alike. Many individuals seek to give women equal standing; however, structural violence—or the normalized and ingrained oppression of women in the marrow of our institutions—means that systems are set in place that do discrimination for us. He said:

> [Men] don't have to wake up in the morning and decide we are going to discriminate against women, because there are religious, political, and social structures already firmly in place that ensure it keeps happening, regardless of whether we consciously do it. My message to young women is that it doesn't have to be this way; it's wrong that it is; and you don't have to put up with it.

My message to young men is that [sitting back and taking advantage of structural violence] is not your prerogative. To the extent you are willing to hitch your wagon to old-fashioned sexism and bigotry that religion, politics, and social systems have made possible, *you're wrong*. You need to act and think differently, and it's your responsibility to live differently than your grandfather, your father, and even the world around you today and the men [in your peer group].[21]

In order for complex religious, political, economic, and cultural institutions to be purged of structural violence, men and boys have to feel empathy for the true humanity of women, relate to the issues, and fully realize what is at stake. Many men hate feminism because they naturally buy into the lie of the hierarchy and its systems, even when the hierarchy does not serve them well either. They fear women speaking up, because they too are insecure in the hierarchy. Their derisiveness, defensiveness, and panic is a misunderstanding of where their own self-worth is derived.

The strongest men are not the ones with power, wealth, and status— wearing designer suits or religious robes. They are the ones who are enlightened and empathic, willing to help others step up to their full potential and support everyone in taking their rightful place, knowing they still have a place too. As Sister Joan Chittister, Benedictine nun and feminist author and lecturer, has said:

Feminism does not come to destroy men. If anything, it comes to save men from imprisonment by a system that cramps the human development of men all the while it purports to give them power. Feminists are not asking men to be less than manly. Feminists are asking women and men not to buy into patriarchal systems that destroy them both. Feminism comes to bring both men and women to the fullness of life, and wholeness of soul for which we were all made "in the image and likeness of God."[22]

What if something other than power-over and masculinity formed the pinnacle of humanness? What if the highest authority in our society was ultimately not about what we have or can hold over others, but rather what we seek?

DEVOTIONAL: **Speaking Sophia**

Wisdom is the apex of human being. Wisdom is equal opportunity; she is power-to. This must be why she disappeared with the rise of the state religion's hierarchy, and why she must be reclaimed as the pinnacle of womanhood.

History, poetry, and art have most famously fashioned women as objects of sexual desire and conquest, alternately admired and exploited. The false pedestal has kept us at the bottom of the hierarchy of power. Yet we know there is a deeper, truer female essence. The Book of Sophia (Greek for *Wisdom*) offers us a female manifestation of God, allowing us to envision the real pinnacle of womanhood.

Some translations used today have removed explicit female references. A translation of the text is called the Book of Wisdom in the Roman Catholic Bible, and called Wisdom of Solomon in the Orthodox Bible, although it was not written by the king of Israel associated with the wisdom sayings of the biblical Proverbs. The musings of King Solomon tended to eroticize the ancient female personification of Wisdom, pursuing her with the intention of making her his wife (he had hundreds), or, in other words, his possession. But in the Book of Sophia, Wisdom stands on her own. She is "primarily bound up with knowledge, rule, teaching, counsel, the most exalted origins, the power to form and create, trustworthiness, salvation, guidance, and virtue, especially justice," says Sophia Wisdom scholar Silvia Schroer.[23] All the things the church fathers said women do not possess and cannot do. "Most of these characteristics are not ordinarily associated with the roles assigned to women in a patriarchal society," Schroer says.

Hebrew in origin, the early Christian fathers rejected the Sophia teachings. But in Proverbs 1—9, written centuries before The Book of Sophia, Wisdom is the savior of humankind. Christians today often believe these references prophesy Jesus, but that interpretation was read back into Hebrew tradition during the establishment of Christian doctrine. In Proverbs 3, Sophia (not Jesus, as the New Testament gospel of John alludes) is the essence through which God created the earth: "The LORD by wisdom founded the earth; / by understanding God established the heavens; / by God's knowledge the deeps broke open" (vv. 19–20a, NRSV). Whereas in the garden of Eden story the tree of knowledge was a deathly threat, its fruit forbidden by God for human consumption, in Proverbs, knowledge is indispensable for creating and sustaining life. It is also the highest priority for human beings who want to live long and prosper: "My child, if you accept my words... / making your ear attentive to wisdom... / then you will...find the knowledge of God... / Long life is in her right hand" (Prov. 2:1a, 2a, 5; 3:16a, NRSV). Woman Wisdom is even called a "*tree of life* to those who lay hold of her; / those who hold her fast are called happy" (Prov. 3:18, NRSV, emphasis mine).

The Book of Sophia was written in the first century B.C.E. when Jews were scattered in Egypt at the onset of Roman rule, where they were denied opportunities and disadvantaged in relation to the hierarchical Hellenistic society.[24] It was a society where "might was the law of right" and a huge gap yawned between the powerful and subjected, the rich and poor. But the trend of individual improvement in social spaces such as the gymnasium sparked Jews to aspire to Greek culture, education, and ideas. This pre-existing Hebrew personification of Wisdom reflected in Proverbs came to life again among some Jews in Alexandria—where certain women had more rights for their time—in the form of the Greek-language Sophia. She was resurrected in parallel to the goddess Isis, who ruled over all cosmic and earthly powers and held destiny in her hands, allowing her to "break through the fatalistic order of the world."[25] She was exhorted to end injustice, tyranny, and wars. She steered ships to safety on the ocean, appeared to prisoners in their dungeon cells, and brought rewards to the just. That sounded like a great idea to the Jews living there at the time.

Sophia resurged through what the Hellenists called *philosophia*, the striving for wisdom. In her new form and context, "she mediates between the strongly ethical dimensions of biblical wisdom teachings with their interest in the just order of things, and the intellectual concept of wisdom of Greek antiquity, which, in turn, concerned itself with the philosophical and ethical search for the highest good and the greatest happiness."[26] Sophia Wisdom is the justice of God for the highest good.

Sophia was said to be the spirit who brought Adam out of his sin; healed the earth after the great flood; and stood within Abraham, Jacob, Joseph, Moses, and other patriarchs to make them honorable before God when they were unable to endure their challenges. This female language, imagery, and symbolism is used to express the belief in an ultimate "reign of God" to come (Book of Sophia 10:10, 14), which later became the mission of Jesus. Without her, the coming reign of God will not come to pass.

Perhaps the fact that girls and women are still largely oppressed at the bottom of the world's hierarchy—and innate female wisdom and contribution is still stifled—is why the realm of God has not manifested on earth today. Schroer says that, in the Book of Sophia:

> Wisdom as a divine agent of salvation and leader of the exodus is called to mind, she unites herself expressly with the collective history of the whole people of Israel. At the same time she transforms the old Jewish traditions, which are newly selected and narrated in "sophialogical" terms. Thus, the striving toward a just

world is assigned to individuals but is also eased by a collective, salvation-historical assurance.[27]

In chapter 16 of the Book of Sophia, a sign of salvation is the serpent, whose strikes take down raging beasts that symbolize tyranny. We talked earlier about the Gnostic tradition that Eve was the serpent, who nodded humanity toward knowledge for the higher good and sustaining of life. This evokes the wisdom Jesus gave his disciples before sending them with his good news out into the land, like "sheep among wolves." Revolutionaries spreading their subversive message through the violent Roman diaspora of the first century were required to "be wise as serpents and innocent as doves" (Mt. 10:16, NRSV). Their purpose was spreading eye-opening knowledge while tempering radical behavior that could land them in the courts or arenas.

In *Dance of the Dissident Daughter,* Sue Monk Kidd is astonished she once missed the strand of Sophia that snakes her way into the New Testament. She points out that in 1 Corinthians 1:23–24 the Greek calls Christ a mixture of the power and wisdom of God.[28] First Corinthians 2:7–8 says, "But we speak God's wisdom [*sophia*], secret and hidden, which God decreed before the ages for our glory. None of the [Roman] rulers of this age understood this; for if they had, they would not have crucified the Lord of glory" (NRSV). Sophia was alive with God before the ages, and she lived again in the resurrection. Some consider her to be the Holy Spirit in the image of the Trinity. And while Jesus was the man they crucified, the Christ was the spiritual combination of both forces—the power and wisdom of God that lived on.

Many theologians likewise detect Sophia in the masculine *Logos* of John 1:1–4. It calls Jesus the word, or divine utterance, of God, using a very similar description to the ancient Hebrew Sophia: existing with God before the world, involved in creation, the vessel through which the earth comes into being. In ancient Hebrew, and later Hebrew Hellenistic society, this was written about Sophia. But, in the New Testament, it seems the fathers embodied her in the male gender.

Regardless of whether or not she was legitimized in traditional Christianity, we have Sophia Wisdom to provide language and imagery for our true purpose from before the beginning of time. Our innate wisdom, value, and contribution has been repressed and defiled, and our female God image has been hidden from us by the Christian hierarchy. But it is still there within us, its beautiful, strong branches ready to be tended and watered, to grow upward and outward. Our tree of knowledge, our tree of life. Life at its fullest for all.

Reflection:

- What wisdom were you innately given, just by being who you are, to bring into the world?
- What principles of goodness and abundant life do you think you were uniquely created to reveal?
- Where does your story entail the pursuit or discovery of wisdom? What have been your big "aha!" moments?
- In what instances or ways have you been poisoned by the denial of your female wisdom by hierarchical society? In what moments have you been silent when you had something to say? How have you, or will you, flip the script?
- What knowledge and truth do you want your life to speak to others and to the world?
- Knowledge, rule, teaching, counsel, the most exalted origins, the power to form and create, trustworthiness, salvation, guidance, virtue, and justice were characteristics ascribed to Sophia. In what ways do you particularly represent these traits and use these abilities in your spiritual practice, personal relationships, and work life?

Meditation: Sophia Wisdom is my birthright. I am the tree of life, branches rising beyond the structures of the world, and rooted deeply in the heart of God.

CHAPTER 6

Being Is Believing

My mouth is a fire escape / the words coming out do not care that they are naked / something is burning in there. — ANDREA GIBSON

If other people do not understand our behavior—so what? Their request that we must only do what they understand is an attempt to dictate to us. If this is being "asocial" or "irrational" in their eyes, so be it. Mostly they resent our freedom and our courage to be ourselves. — ERICH FROMM

Only she who attempts the absurd can achieve the impossible.

—ROBIN MORGAN

"I started questioning gender-based assumptions a long time ago," says Emma Watson, the actress famous for her role as Hermione in the Harry Potter movie series. Watson spoke in September 2014 at the United Nations headquarters in New York City for the launch of UN Women's HeForShe campaign, a solidarity movement involving men to work for gender equality.[1] During her speech, Watson shared some of her reasons for being a feminist. At age eight, she was maligned as "bossy" because she wanted to direct a play her friends were putting on for their parents. The boys were expected to direct, and without being called names for wanting to. When she was fourteen, the media began to hyper-sexualize her, despite the fact that she was (and is) a disciplined, mature, serious actor. At fifteen, she noticed her female friends dropping out of participation in sports, afraid of developing too much muscle.

Watson's speech was lauded, went viral, and resonated with many. But within 24 hours, misogynists were threatening to release fake nude photos of her online, and started rumors she had died. The patriarchal machine launched its inevitable, hateful campaign to intimidate and shame her into silence, as it does to every woman who speaks out. Being labeled "bossy" instead of having your leadership skills recognized and respected. Being twisted into a sexual object despite your professionalism. Forsaking your athletic ability and potential to conform to a male-constructed body ideal. Sexism splits us in two, separates us from who we were created to be, and isolates us from our purpose.

Our faith traditions should not further pry apart our being from our believing—whether in ourselves or in God. Our experience of being women in the world should align with the God of freedom and justice in whom we believe. Our faith should propel us to speak up and make change, not shrink and succumb.

Have you ever felt split between two worlds and two versions of yourself: the real you in your real life, and the religious or spiritual you? We often blame ourselves for that split—for not praying enough, not being righteous enough, not going through the right motions. But our real life and our faith life are one and the same, no matter how messy, bumpy, and imperfect. Practicing faith is not about becoming a perfect spiritual being who hovers above it all; it is about being the best of who we are and not being ashamed. It is getting our hands dirty working to make this world a place where we all have the opportunity to be our best. Doing this work to bring a new realm of equality is the practice of our faith.

Erich Fromm, the famous German-born psychoanalyst and social philosopher in the U.S. in the 1940s–1970s, wrote *The Art of Being* around the realization that becoming a whole person must be the supreme goal of life if we are to experience well-being and reach our full potential. Fromm wrote the book in response to increasing consumerism, in consideration of the question, "To have or to be?" He looked at how the ego keeps us trapped in the quest to *have* things, while our ability to be spiritually fulfilled through purposeful *being* begins to atrophy. He asserted that love, reason, and productive, meaningful work are what truly make up our being. We must unlearn what we have been taught to the contrary, and relearn how to authentically be within systems that try to get us to do self-sabotaging things in support of profits and power-over. In *The Anatomy of Human Destructiveness,* Fromm affirms that what it means to have faith is the opposite of simply believing what we are told. Faith, according to Fromm, is not separate from our innate drive and desire for self-actualization:

> To have faith means to dare, to think the unthinkable, yet to act within the limits of the realistically possible; it is the paradoxical hope to expect the Messiah every day, yet not to lose heart when he has not come at the appointed hour. This hope is not passive and it is not patient; on the contrary, it is impatient and active, looking for every possibility of action within the realm of real possibilities.

Least of all it is passive as far as the growth and liberation of one's own person are concerned.[2]

One is not required to subscribe to Fromm's Buddhist sensibilities, or his background as an Orthodox Jew who later gravitated to Christian mysticism, or his interpretations of Freud and Marx, to appreciate his point about how easily we are convinced to forsake our own wholeness in order to fit in or be accepted. We daily forfeit our belief in who we are out of loyalty to institutions that eat away at us while claiming to improve us, complete us, defend us, or save us. Advertising for everything from beauty products to banking to political candidates convinces us to believe what corporations and institutions say about us and buy into their version of reality.

Jesus admonished his followers to break loyalty to overbearing systems to pursue healing and wholeness as part of what he called the "realm of God." Entering a new realm of dignity and potential requires leaving the status-quo comfort zone behind. Theologian Elisabeth Schüssler Fiorenza exhorts us: "As a feminist vision, the *basileia* [Greek for *kingdom, realm, rule*] vision of Jesus calls all women without exception to wholeness and selfhood."[3] We are called to work toward this way of being, but, unfortunately, the powerful old structures of our society and religion make it quite a challenge. In his *Escape from Freedom*, Fromm talks about the fear of freedom that can haunt human beings who have been subject for so long that autonomy and choice feel like a daunting burden. He writes in 1941 about the history of European social conditions between the Middle Ages and the twentieth century—conditions that eventually paved a way for the rise of the Nazi Party in Germany.

Fromm explores, from a psychological perspective, why the German people supported Hitler's totalitarian regime. He cites the alienation, amidst social and economic change, that was prevalent among the masses, who had graduated slowly, over a few generations, from the strict overlording of Roman Catholicism to the ripples of the Reformation. People were now allowed to worship God directly, but the doctrines of Luther and Calvin were teaching them that humanity, being intrinsically corrupt and depraved, must work to receive salvation from a vindictive, punishing God. The working classes had also begun to enjoy direct employment by capital holders, but as a consequence were losing familial and personal ties to vocations, and their intimate personal roles and healthy community interdependency.[4]

With the spread of capitalism that sprouted from the Protestant Reformation, life was quickly becoming "every man for himself."[5] The resulting isolation, Fromm assessed, left a gap for Hitler to exploit the ongoing uncertainty and struggle of managing newfound freedoms, no matter how modest or incremental. Hitler and his regime presented a way for people to escape the pressures of steep learning curves and the risk of failure by depending upon and submitting to a strong leader who promised to march their society to glory and victory over the competitors looming in a shrinking globe.[6]

We live in a different environment today, but for women undergoing their first experience of isolation from the "rewards" and "protections" of being good girls for the patriarchy, the disorientation is a threat. When we leave the old belief structure behind, we enter a free fall; we are suddenly dependent on no one but ourselves, yet we have not been taught how to fight for ourselves, believe in our abilities, trust our instincts and decisions, appreciate and love our bodies, and demand respect. This leaves an opportunity for maleficent forces to convince us we need and want the wrong kind of victories, assisted by the wrong kind of heroes. It makes getting "rescued" by Prince Charming seem like the best option. As Sue Monk Kidd has said, "When a woman starts to disentangle herself from patriarchy, ultimately she is abandoned to her own self."[7] It can be scary and lonely.

It was a golden-lit October afternoon, exactly one month to the day after the strange meeting with the future-telling fashionista in the Chelsea nail salon. I was running late for a table reading of a play I was in, and I hustled up the sidewalk, weaving my way through the crowds. I had to stop to pick up an allergy prescription or else I would sneeze through the rehearsal. I was focused on my mission, and cleared a row of pumpkins with a little leap in order to shortcut to the drugstore's front door. Exiting at the same time was a petite, pony-tailed young mother laden with shopping bags, pushing her crying baby in a stroller and clutching the hand of her small, wriggly toddler. She was distracted managing her brood, and I swerved around her to avoid plowing into her. I took maybe three more steps before I heard a voice cry, "Miss!" It sounded urgent, like someone collapsing beneath bags and babies.

"Miss, please!" I turned around and our eyes locked. She didn't seem to care that her little boy was pulling violently at her arm or that her toiletries were spilling onto the sidewalk. We stood just inside the store's entranceway, the electronic doors jumping robotically as we held the laser movement detector hostage. The setting sun streamed in brightly from behind her, and I had to push my sunglasses onto my head to see her face.

"This is going to sound strange," she said in a calm, hushed voice, "but I need to tell you something." With both arms in danger of being pulled out of socket, holding the stroller and the spinning toddler behind her, she went on to recite a shorter version of the same speech the woman in the nail salon had delivered: *You have been silenced by suppositions. You are on a difficult journey. You must find your voice because there is something that needs to be said, something people need to hear. You must pay attention, and come to know and trust yourself. You have to be brave; it matters.*

Agitated and confused, and still in a very big hurry, I pushed my sunglasses back down onto my nose and mumbled, "I am in a serious rush." Embarrassed at my own rudeness, I turned and made haste toward the pharmacy in the back. The nice Southern girl was starting to get frustrated and defensive. "I'm not trying to scare you," her voice trailed after me, as if she could see right through me. "I just could not leave this store without saying what God asked me to. I wish you well." *God again? Really? What the hell?* I did not look back. But exactly one month later, after Thanksgiving dinner, I peered skeptically into an idling cab, opened the door, and unwittingly slid into what felt like an alternate reality. And I ended up in free fall on my foyer floor.

All these years later, I look back and wonder what would have happened if I had not been afraid. What would I have done differently then if I had believed what those strange messengers said about me? What would you be capable of doing if you could clearly see and believe the truth about yourself, and feel supported by the universe in your purpose? What if we were not split in two—our being from our believing?

At that point, I would not have recognized a God who would encourage my authentic voice or allow me to honestly vocalize everything I experienced. I did not know anything about a God who would want me to recognize I had divine Sophia Wisdom inside me. I had not yet detected, as Paul Tillich would say, "the God above theism."

The romantic longing for fate to swoop in and commence our happily-ever-after is really a convenient way for us to evade the pain of making strange new choices, hard calls, scary changes, and questionable left turns. But the only other option is facing the isolation and disorientation that comes with setting aside fairy tales and Bible stories as maps to our futures, and forging our own paths, led by the voice of God within us. As Sue Monk Kidd says:

> There is no place so awake and alive as the edge of becoming. But more than that, birthing the kind of woman who can authentically say, "My soul is my own," and then embody it in her life, her spirituality, and her community is worth the risk and hardship.[8]

The edge of becoming. That is where we feel most alive, find authentic purpose, and push ourselves to the next level of hope, bravery, and action. We know we are on to something when, every day, being is a process of constant becoming. So, how do we ignite a faith practice in which our being and becoming is the expression and manifestation of our belief? The key, perhaps surprisingly, lies in our frustrations. I don't mean your feelings when your significant other leaves dirty socks on the floor or your mother criticizes your outfit. I mean frustrations about the way the world operates.

Carter Heyward, feminist theologian and lesbian Episcopal priest, was one of the "Philadelphia Eleven," the eleven original women whose ordinations made it possible for women to be recognized as priests in the Episcopal Church in 1976. My favorite piece of advice Heyward offers is this: *Let your frustration guide you.* It will lead you to your life's purpose, and it will benefit a lot of people and change the status quo along the way.

If nothing is frustrating you, you may want to either look around a little more or check your pulse. If we pay attention to what truly frustrates us, we come to know what is important to us. In the book *Missing Out: In Praise of the Unlived Life,* professor and psychoanalyst Adam Phillips lays out his theory on the importance of the frustration we encounter in the gap between our lived lives and our unlived lives. Our lived lives are our actual lives—warts and all. Our unlived lives—visions of the lives that we could have had or still hope to attain—can haunt us, reminding us that our needs have not been met or our desires have not been fulfilled despite our longing. If we let it, our reverence for the dream of the unlived life can make us feel like we are constantly falling short. But, Phillips asks, "What happens if we remove the idea of failure from the equation?"[9] Phillips advises that we take frustration to be a gift rather than a curse. Only upon identifying what affects us negatively, what is lacking, and what an alternate reality would look like, do we generate a vision. And then suddenly satisfaction is conceivable, and the new reality has potential to come into being.

It is surprisingly difficult, says Phillips, to allow ourselves to actually experience our frustration. We have multiple mechanisms of pain avoidance and delusion that offer us the option to skip blindly along our way. In some religious traditions, we are not supposed to feel frustrated, unless we are not doing something right or somehow deserve it. This is especially impressed upon women, who are called to be content, patient, and sadistically "forgiving." We explain frustrating things away by saying it is God's plan, or a trial by which God is testing our mettle or measuring our faithfulness. We say it all works together for our good, even when it does not, and even when ignoring it doesn't work for anyone's good.

Jesus was frustrated a lot, and it propelled his mission. All four canonized gospels recount the time he went ballistic in the temple, turning over the tables of the money-changers. He cracked a whip at the merchants, who in collusion with the ruling powers took advantage of people's commitment to religious practices, forcing them to spend their meager means to appease God, and cheating them in the process. For Jesus, the consumerizing of souls would not do. So he drove them all out—such was the force of his frustration and anger.

If we desire to truly follow the way of Jesus, the faithful and evolved thing to do is to override those mechanisms of suppression and tune in, trusting that our instincts are saying something meaningful. If we will go there, and allow ourselves to learn to be with our "potentially productive forms of ordinary frustrations,"[10] we realize they are a source of both rewarding engagement and inspiration for our unlived lives.

One last thing: Keep in mind that this attention to being with our frustration is never a call to accept mistreatment or abuse. To the contrary, it is the call to identify and free ourselves from it, with an eye toward ending it on behalf of others too. It is active, not passive, frustration that energizes change.

Spiritual Being as Believing

Andrea Gibson is not gentle with her truths, which is one reason she has emerged at the forefront of the spoken word movement, winning the first Women of the World Poetry Slam in 2008. Gibson's heart-ripping fusion of stark reality with deep empathy puts flesh on the bones of the concept that being is believing. Her frustrations become lyrical magic. Our spiritual being-as-believing means calling the world like it is and not being afraid to viscerally describe its real-world effects on us or others in terms that leave an impression. It is poetry as protest, embodied exposition, a living testament. In a poem called "Thank Goodness," Gibson, an engaging voice of the gay community, interrogates religion's tendency to split us apart and smack us down to uphold a lie about holiness:

I've seen too many prayers
caught in the grills of eighteen-wheelers.
Folks like us, we may have shoulder blades that rust in the rain
but they're still G-sharp
whenever our spinal chords are tuned
to the key of redemption.
So go ahead, world, pick us
to make things better.[11]

Redemption is not what we've been told it is. Redemption has to start with recognizing who we really are instead of denying it, and then giving that identity a voice. It is not about killing off our former selves; it is about growing them up out of the earthy grass, always rising. The people who religion claims have nothing to say are the ones who should be talking, who will "word" us into wakeful being.

Our spirituality is our conviction awake and in action. German liberation theologian Dorothee Soelle wrote *The Silent Cry: Mysticism and Resistance* to dispel the assumption that heady spirituality is physically stationary or tangibly impotent. Mysticism entails a union with God through quiet contemplation, but that should, in turn, lead to vocalization and movement. Contemplation leads to intuition of truths that transcend an ordinary, everyday understanding of the world.[12] What we then do with it is the purpose of it all. To change the world, we have to embody our spirituality and be the wisdom that comes to us. We have to act upon it.

"For mystical consciousness," Soelle says, "it is essential that everything internal become external and be made visible. A dream wants to be told, the 'inner light' wants to shine, the vision has to be shared."[13] This is crucial, since Soelle identifies the suppression of this kind of transcendent externalizing as the primary weapon society uses to cut off Sophia Wisdom and women's contributions from the world:

> The trivialization of women exists as an ongoing malevolent belittling: whatever is consistently and without opposition declared to be irrelevant—like so much that women experience, feel, and come to know—loses its language; perhaps it may echo for a while within a person, but it creates no response...
>
> Such dreams and ideas are therefore of no consequence and the inner light is rationalized away. It is so easy to douse the inner light of a human being... We cut ourselves off from our own experiences by looking upon them as irrelevant and not worth talking about or, what is no less cynical, not communicable at all. We are losing dreams...and increasingly we lose the visions of our life.[14]

In our culture, one example of the belittling suppression Soelle describes is when men address each other as "girls" or "ladies" to reduce each other in status or show a lack of respect for one another. In a television commercial for AFLAC insurance, a football coach calls the players in a locker room "ladies" to establish his authority over them. There's a commercial for Summer's Eve feminine body wash in which the husband accidentally uses the product, then feels so disgusted and compromised that he is compelled to frantically do as many stereotypically "manly" activities as possible to reverse any adverse effect on his strength as a man. The last line of the commercial, uttered by the wife, is, "That was close!" Now, why would a company that makes and profits from intimate products for women bet that scenes about a man feeling humiliated by using it would convince women they need it?[15] That is the discouraging depth of the buy-in.

This seemingly innocuous but slangy way men talk about women is another pervasive example of the insidious, socially accepted structural violence that Galen Guengerich was talking about earlier. Little boys and little girls pick it up and believe that females are weak and less-than. Worse, it makes it impossible—or at least socially dangerous—for boys to identify with girls and develop empathy for us, because they do not want to be a "pussy," or inferior to the male standard. The view of the vagina as pathetic, helpless, and so low as to be an insult to men perpetuates the rape culture. This is a culture in which men put women "in our place" by exerting male power over us by violating us sexually. (Rape is often not about sex, it is about power-over and the perpetrator asserting his male rank.) When men belittle each other with the term "pussy," it means the perceived weaker males are exhibiting "feminine" behavior that other men translate into "asking for it," to be roughed up. If you think deeply into the historic, symbolic phenomenon of men (and women!) using this term, it is truly disturbing. It also takes us right back to the misinterpretation of Eve as weak and evil, and the punishment womankind was imagined to have deserved: being lorded over by men forever, and enduring the pain of childbirth. But Soelle reminds us that mysticism—the true expression of our spiritual being—is a form of resistance:

> In the face of this actual condition of repression, faith and hope do not function within a depoliticized, privatized piety but in a historically novel combination of kneeling down and learning to walk upright. These two movements, kneeling down and standing up, belong together and succeed only in tandem.[16]

We may sit to meditate, recline to visualize, or kneel to pray; however, in so doing, we gain the vision and power to unfold and stand up straight and strong. We gain the necessary momentum to speak and act on behalf of our freedom. The faith, hope, internal awareness, and centered focus that are strengthened by quiet contemplation—in other words, our spiritual being—are potent weapons against trivialization and discrimination. If we do not act on our contemplative wisdom, we have gained no wisdom at all.

The eye of the mystic homes in on God at work in the world, and, following the way of Jesus with the wisdom of Sophia, joins in with everything she is.

Physical Being as Believing

To "embody" means to give a bodily or tangible form to an abstract concept. It is to bring an intuitive construct into being, to make an ideal incarnate.[17] To embody something is to be an example of that idea or principle. It's what Sophia and Jesus did, becoming one human being who brought God's wisdom and power to earth, to turn us on to what a different reality could look like and how it could take shape.

Mahatma Gandhi was said to have given a charge that later was whittled down to a slogan: *Be the change you wish to see in the world.* But for women, embodying our ideals is not so simple. Our bodies already carry a certain, seemingly inescapable meaning in the world. This dynamic holds us prisoner to power-over. To be frank, it's hard to be the change when all the energy and interest is focused on our "tits and ass." Whether it's street harassment[18], people in our social circles, people in the workplace, or forces in the media, the commentary on women's bodies is constant. Sometimes it feels as if the collective eye of society owns the female body, instead of each one of us owning our own. Our physicality as women is public domain.

If you have never seen Jean Kilbourne's "Killing Us Softly" series of documentaries about the negative consequences that exploitative images of women in advertising and media have on our psyches and lives—I highly recommend exploring jeankilbourne.com. In the trailer for Killing Us Softly 4, she talks about how ads sell values; gender roles; and concepts of love, sexuality, family, lifestyle, and success. In addition to the rampant use of Photoshop to alter photographs to whittle away weight and imperfections, Kilbourne also exposes the fact that we have been raised in a culture that automatically turns women's bodies into *things.*

Not content with just morphing us into flesh and blood sex objects, we are also meshed with other inanimate objects of desire for men, such as cars, games, and beer bottles.[19] An ad for Ché men's magazine shows a practically naked young woman sprawled seductively on a bed with the chord of a video game controller emerging from her belly button. She is reclining on the bed in wait of a man—any man—to come "play her." The caption says, "Keep on dreaming of a better world." Yes, this is what advertisers who cater to male spending power are telling guys they should aspire to: controlling a naked, helpless fembot to do whatever you want her to do. This image is only one of many that ups the game of power-over.

Girls are toys at your disposal, and you have the controls. And, for these men, and all the boys they are influencing, this is how the world "should be."

Kilbourne points out that turning a human being into a thing is almost always the first step toward justifying violence against that person. When someone is dehumanized—moreover, by popular, trusted brands in "clever" ways—violence becomes inevitable. It is not necessarily a direct result of one particular ad, but as minds are inundated with impression after impression, the idea becomes normalized and within reach. This explains why the teenage football players in Steubenville, Ohio—who had supposedly been raised well by attentive parents—would rape a passed-out young girl, dragging her lifeless body around like a rag doll while making jokes about her and filming her on camera phones.[20] And why others stood around and let it go on. We must understand there are many forces at work to teach boys (and girls) what females are made for, suggesting that women exist to be used and are "asking" to be "consumed."

Another popular ad style involves only showing a woman's breasts, torso, rear, or legs in the ad, with no head or face attached. We don't even think twice when we see these disconnected body parts; society thinks of dismembered women in ads as normal. But the message over time and assimilation is that a woman is just parts available for purchase, enjoyment, and entertainment—not a whole and conscious human being with a head (and a brain), much less a purpose. Epidemic levels of eating disorders, domestic violence, and sexual assault are unsurprising. "These are public health problems that affect us all," says Kilbourne. She also says on her website: "Action is the antidote to despair."

Perhaps at some point in our generation, we will realize that attempting to "take back" our physical being by choosing to act out the over-the-top male sexual construct we have been tied to—for instance, the recently mainstreamed male-dominant porn aesthetic—is not really taking anything back. It is actually giving in to a deep need for acceptance by what we mistake as our own volition.

At what point in history will we stop and figure out what our genuine sexuality looks and feels like? When do we get to make it about our own fulfillment, instead of the male gaze? At what point do we boldly break out of this old structure and use our imaginations to construct a new reality? When do we focus on being something else entirely—upping the game for all of us, across gender lines and expressions? At this point in history, women have played every character, and tried to co-opt or claim every form of male power. We are starting to see this only gets us so far, because our responses have followed pre-established, male-centric rules that take us in circles, and we always end up back at the beginning, playing to male fantasy. We must create a new paradigm if we want to really belong to ourselves.

Our purpose is not to judge others' choices; our purpose is to better understand all the choices available to us, including the ones we have not tried or do not even know about yet. We have to think carefully about what we choose to embody. I know from my own mistakes that some choices only feed the monster that blindly consumes women's flesh with impersonal and insatiable voracity. Sadly, despite our best intentions, some choices keep our navels plugged into game consoles. As I personally struggle with these nuanced decisions about physical being, I always go back to Jacqui Lewis' observation (found in chapter 2): "Women must be conscious that our testifying is transformative, shaping a new narrative." Everything about us is a form of testifying—our bodies, our voices, our personalities, our movements. Not necessarily to who we are—because we all mistakenly, or under pressure and anxiety, or even under normalized expectations, do things that are untrue to ourselves. But what we embody is a testament to who we *believe* we are, to who we believe we can become. Our testimony creates a narrative and a reality we will have to live in. And others will live in it, too.

Feminism is about creating choices for women without the threat of coercion or judgment. But with that also comes a huge responsibility for every choice we make—to pause and consider how it affects every other woman in the world—from the ones who are similar to us to those who cannot get an education, who are brutalized daily, and who are barely surviving in the most horrific situations imaginable.[21] Our unlived lives are bound with blood ties. Until we all can manifest that ideal life, none of us can take it for granted.

Being with One Another

"Embodiment means we no longer say, I had this experience; we say, I am this experience," observes Sue Monk Kidd.[22] When we practice embodiment, we own what we believe. We become what we believe. We own what we go through, what we learn; we make it all part of ourselves, both positive and negative. We reach out and get help with our traumas and work on healing, but we never abandon what we need to remember, what others need to know, and the difficult stories that will change our world. We become more beautiful, more admirable, more real, more faithful, and more effective. We have more to offer.

Biblical scholar Renita Weems wrote *Showing Mary: How Women Can Share Prayers, Wisdom, and the Blessings of God* based on the story that Mary, upon learning she was pregnant with Jesus, went to stay with her older cousin Elizabeth, who was also pregnant. Weems sees this action on Mary's part as a symbol of God's greater provision for females, which ideally comes in the care and presence of other women.[23] Being, learning, and fortifying ourselves in the midst of other women is something society finds suspicious, and thus is a gift from which we are often discouraged. In our day and time, with our overbooked schedules and short attention spans, it can also be hard to arrange—which, of course, are all reasons why it is important for us to intentionally claim one another this way, even if we have to do it via untraditional methods.

I was once in a Lenten prayer group with several women via a Google group. We all lived in New York City or the boroughs, but it proved impossible to find times and places to physically get together. Across cyber space and over a couple of years, the bond we developed and our support of one another was visceral. We shared our intimate personal journeys via e-mail through those forty days, praying for and encouraging one another from mobile phones and laptops through the season of darkness and contemplation to the hope of Easter. We were all very different women— ages, races, families, hometowns, careers, goals, and religious traditions. But we discovered much that we shared: painful experiences, abuses, haunting memories, bad choices, and big mistakes, plus some enormous discoveries, successes, and triumphs. These had made us who we are. Weems advises cultivating a diverse range of friends from all walks of life, ages, and backgrounds. Our faith is not about being just like everyone around us. Conformity is the antithesis of being-as-believing.

We are doing the spiritual equivalent of growing up as we practice, and we need all the history, perspective, and substance we can get. We don't need role models to show us how to keep performing patriarchal roles well. We need models of real, grounded, healthy female being.

"Don't just choose your friends by those who will encourage you and tell you what you want to hear," Weems says. "Find a friend who will love you enough to tell you the truth as she sees it."[24] We need to be lovingly challenged by one another in a way that enhances our faith and expands our being. Weems encourages us not to listen to just anyone, but to "go find Elizabeth"—one or more dependable, thoughtful co-journeyers with whom we can exchange experiences and wisdom.

Weems gives us a poem-prayer to help call more of these relationships into our lives:

Whoever Elizabeth is, she is not far from where I am right at this
    moment.

Show her to me. Show me to her. Show us to each other.

I thank you for the loyalty and the love of the Elizabeths I already
    have in my life.

Deepen those bonds so we might continue to grow together.

But for the secret parts of me that are on the verge of being born,

send new Elizabeths to help midwife them and show me how to do
    the same for them.

God, I am ready.[25]

This Is Your Brain on Belief

Being ready is something we have to notice and act upon, even though
readiness is an innate condition that grows as we cultivate it. In the book
Why God Won't Go Away: Brain Science and the Biology of Belief, the authors
use scientific research on the brain to explore the nature of consciousness
and the phenomenon of spirituality, to connect the dots between faith and
reason, mysticism and action, through data. As much as they can be, these
are traced through advances in the field of neurotheology, which explores
the intersection of science and religion, and specifically the relationship
between the brain and theology, the mind and spirituality.[26]

The research involved imaging the brains of advanced spiritual
practitioners while they meditated or prayed, via injected single photon
emission computed tomography cameras. The studies led the researchers
to the conclusion that the brain is naturally wired for spiritual experience,
and even creates it. There is a bit of chicken-or-egg about the genesis,
which actually makes sense being that we experience everything in the
same mind in which it is generated and perceived. Spiritual experience, or
being spiritual, is "intimately interwoven with human biology. That biology,
in some way, compels the spiritual urge."[27] In other words, the brain and
belief are not at odds, and actually nor are science and spirituality. I'll spare
you all the brain science now, but one particular nugget in the research
brings us back to our intuitive, experiential connection to God:

Our minds are drawn by the intuition of this deeper reality, this
utter sense of oneness, where suffering vanishes and all desires are
at peace. As long as our brains are arranged the way they are,
as long as our minds are capable of sensing this deeper reality,
spirituality will continue to shape the human experience, and God,
however we define that majestic, mysterious concept, will not go
away.[28]

Andrew Newburg, the lead author of *Why God Won't Go Away*, found that spiritual practices can help shape and change our brains for the better, making us more focused, attentive, and aware. Even more important is that our spirituality is opened to encompass all that we are, and all of the unique experiences our brains process and which shape our conscious minds and form our reality. We are all wired with a sense of the spiritual; yet our environment, upbringing, education, cultural experiences, and other stimuli in our surroundings direct us toward a certain expression (or suppression) of it that becomes familiar and rote. Our upbringing often defines the manifestation of our drive for the spiritual. We come to think of that as right, and perhaps the only way. But there is no one right way to embody and practice our beliefs, other than what comes naturally to each of us. The challenge is to get back to what is natural for us as women, after centuries of being held captive to the male religious construct.

While traditional religious practice is often scripted for a certain place or space, many of us locate our most intense spirituality when our bodies move outside of ecclesial walls. My friend Katerina experiences God when she runs. She says it feels like God's spirit is with her and moving in her, and it feels like prayer. I have had the same experience as a ballet dancer, using my body as an instrument to tell a story. Many find it in yoga, where the mind is calmed and the body is moved to the rhythm of the breath. There is a real phenomenon of feeling close to God when we use our bodies athletically and artistically, when we connect to our breath and its animating spirit. We get the feeling of God's pleasure, not at our achievements, promotions, positions, educations, or salaries, but simply at our being.

Your spiritual practice could include horseback riding, hiking, swimming, rowing, scuba diving, or skating. It could be hitting a baseball, dunking a basketball, or doing a gymnastics routine. It could be sewing, writing music, drawing and designing, or housecleaning. We don't have to go somewhere authorized and do the same old things to worship, to be spiritually renewed, or to commune with God. Our brains and bodies are equally present in our spirituality, and our traditions have too long tried to leave both of them out.

But where is the heart of being? Doctors have recently come to know a lot more about the role the heart plays in leading our brains to establish our sense of being. Dr. Joel Kahn, a Clinical Professor of Medicine at Wayne State University and Director of Cardiac Wellness at Michigan Healthcare Professionals PC, wrote an article about this for *Mind, Body, Green*. He says the fibrous muscle that pumps blood through our bodies to all our organs has some 40,000 sensory neurons that relay information from the heart to the brain (not the other way around). In fact, via nervous system connections, hormones the heart itself produces, biomechanical data carried via blood pressure, and strong electrical and electromagnetic fields, more information is sent daily from the heart to the brain than vice versa. Some of the leading researchers in the burgeoning field of neurocardiology even call the heart "the little brain."[29]

The idea that the heart feels love, joy, pain, and transcendent connection is not just a fanciful old tale. And this feeling heart is not a hypothetical, fuzzy figment outside of the physical heart; it is not something we made up to explain the deep emotions that emanate from our chests. Dr. Kahn says the heart is able to "learn, remember, and make decisions independent of the brain's cerebral cortex" via its network of neurons.[30] We really do learn things by heart, and it is a whole other level of knowing.

Our hearts emit a surrounding electrical field that is sixty times more amplified than the brain's activity, with an electromagnetic field 5,000 times stronger. It can be measured anywhere on our bodies (not just at the heart site) by an EKG, but also can be measured several feet outside the body. People who are a within a few feet of each other (even a human and her pet) actually show brain activity that measures the energy of the heart of the other, such is the powerful interaction of the electromagnetic energy of our hearts.

This is why sometimes we recognize such strong vibes around certain people, or can sense things that are never said; it is why we experience intuition. Our heart-energy makes us all clairvoyant about those to whom we come close in proximity, if we pay attention. We also literally take things to heart, and are affected deeply by energy that we feel from others. Perhaps most important for our practice of being as believing, Dr. Kahn says the electrical activity of the heart and brain can "be guided into a synchronous electrical rhythm easily measured and displayed by simply focusing on positive and loving emotions emanating from the heart."[31] This means a few things.

First, as we concentrate on being as believing, we should follow one cliché, and always listen to our hearts. More than ever we know it will not steer us wrong. But we cannot wait for it to be forced to scream at us in crisis to wake us up. We must tend to it every day, by whichever methods work best. Whether we tune in by meditation, prayer, song, or physical activity, we must take the voice of the heart seriously. It is the still, small voice of God.

Second, we know in concrete, biological terms that we can decide in our hearts to be a certain way—we can envision, believe, and embody our unlived life. We can practice this in our spiritual engagement of our brains and bodies. We can work daily toward being whole and unified, and then use that ability to strengthen ties with each other. We have great power-to tools in our electromagnetic fields emanating and intermingling with God and those around us. This carries real power. It gives new meaning to Jesus' greatest commandments to love God with all our hearts and minds, and to love others as we love ourselves.

Finally, we must intentionally go out of our way to fill our hearts with strong, loving, productive, positive, nurturing, affirming, and female-supportive things—be they images, words, scriptures, sayings, prayers, mantras, groups, or activities. This is why women must have a nonviolent, peaceful, righteously pissed-off, idealistic, equality-driven, loving God to commune with outside the boundaries of the patriarchal church system: what we hold in our hearts makes up our very being.

DEVOTIONAL: Heart Vision

Lectio divina [Latin *divine reading*] is a tool we can use to practice being-as-believing by learning to let God speak to us in an unmediated way through our senses and experiences, evoked by reading a text. The ancient practice brings a text alive in a meditation-like process that allows us to encounter God in our own unique way. "Our memories, images, and feelings become an important context for experiencing God's voice active in us, and we discover it when we pray from our hearts," says Christine Valters Paintner in her book *Lectio Divina—The Sacred Art: Transforming Words and Images into Heart-Centered Prayer*.[32]

This is a heart-centered endeavor. Our minds will want to think about the words we select, control the process, and analyze or judge what comes up. But the reason it is called a practice is because it takes practice! The goal is to let go and let our hearts meet God without all the old assumptions that get in the way. "The heart is the place of receptivity, integration, and meaning-making," Valters Paintner says. "It is where thinking, feeling, intuition, and wisdom come together."[33]

Valters Paintner's approach to *lectio divina* reflects the need to call our true selves into being with a wide variety of material, including our own lives, and not limit ourselves to the canonized biblical texts or patriarchal writings. She prays not only with scripture, but with "art, music, poetry, dreams, nature, and life experience."[34] She gets that some of us encounter the holy *everywhere other* than the traditional, formal places. The four main elements to praying *lectio divina* in Valters Paintner's practice include:

- Being present with and attentive to your breath, letting go of distractions.
- Noticing the images, physical sensations, feelings, and memories that are evoked by the words on which you choose to focus.
- Quietly listening to your inner response to the words, and the impact or awareness that it brings.
- Releasing those thoughts, images, and associations; then resting in inner stillness with God.

To begin, choose a text you are interested in: a passage from a book, a poem, the lyrics to a song, a chapter of scripture—it can be anything. Read it through at least twice. See what word, phrase, or sentence jumps out of the passage and speaks to you, unsettles you, intrigues you, or beckons to your unlived life. Repeat this word or phrase to yourself several times, either out loud or in silence. Then read the full text again, and turn your specific word or phrase over in your imagination and reflect on it deeply. Engage all of your senses with it, and notice what sights, sounds, smells, and tastes are evoked. Make it as vivid as possible. What feelings arise? What memories and experiences come up? Try not to make assessments, excuses, or arguments about what comes up, just notice and let it be what it is. This is hard, but will get easier with time.

Read the full text once more. Is there an awareness coming to you in relationship to your particular word or phrase? An invitation drawing you to explore further? Is your intuition stirring? Are you getting a feeling in your heart? If not, it is perfectly okay. If so, think about what it might mean for your experience of being and believing, for yourself and for the world around you. Now transition into stillness, slow your reflections, deepen your breath, and be fully present in your body. Spend a few moments just resting and cultivating gratitude and love, simply being with the presence of God. As thoughts fight to stay around, keep letting them go, and return to a focus on breathing in and out. Let joy at your simple state of being rise and emanate from your heart, through your entire body, into your mind, and out into the world.

Below are a few suggested texts for *lectio divina* practice. Or you can go back and use what you wrote about your personal myth or your "I Am" statements in earlier devotionals. The lyrics to India Arie's "Soulbird Rise" are another option.

The quality of light by which we scrutinize our lives has direct bearing upon the product which we live, and upon the changes which we hope to bring about through those lives. It is within this light that we form those ideas by which we pursue our magic and make it realized. This is poetry as illumination, for it is through poetry that we give name to those ideas which are—until the poem—nameless and formless, about to be birthed, but already felt. That distillation of experience from which true poetry springs births thought as dream births concept, as feeling births idea, as knowledge births (precedes) understanding.

—AUDRE LORDE, FROM THE ESSAY "POETRY IS NOT A LUXURY"[35]

This is the way of those who hold something of the immeasurable greatness from above. They stretch toward the full one alone, who is a Mother for them. They do not descend into Hades nor do they have envy or groaning. They do not have death within themselves, but they rest in the one who rests. They are not troubled or twisted around the truth, but they are the truth.

—THE GOSPEL OF TRUTH 27:1–5[36]

No mirror ever became iron again; No bread ever
became wheat; No ripened grape ever became
sour fruit. Mature yourself and be secure from a
change for the worse. Become Light.

—RUMI, MATHNAWI II, 1317–18[37]

CHAPTER 7

She's Got the Whole World in Her Hands

I am convinced that discrimination against women and girls is one of the world's most serious, all-pervasive and largely ignored violations of basic human rights.—JIMMY CARTER

You can't solve a problem using the same thinking that created it.

—ALBERT EINSTEIN

The role of the artist is exactly the same as the role of the lover. If I love you, I have to make you conscious of the things you don't see.

—JAMES BALDWIN

To be clairvoyant means to have the power of seeing things and meanings beyond the accepted range of natural vision. The word in French literally means "clear-sighted."[1] It also refers to being visionary, intuitive, empathic, and prophetic. It wasn't until the mid-nineteenth century that the term took on an indication of incredible psychic abilities, sometimes literally not credible. At its core, true "clear-sightedness" is not about magic, fortune-telling, or deception. It is about how we employ our sight, its level of intensity, and our ability to see what is happening around us and what is coming. We can use our five senses to assess situations, but if we pay attention to the world around us and listen to our hearts, we all have a sixth sense that will give us more information—a feeling about things, a nudge. We will come to know what is correct. And we will know what to do.

When he came to Nazareth, where he had been brought up, he went to the synagogue on the sabbath day, as was his custom. He stood up to read, and the scroll of the prophet Isaiah was given to him. He unrolled the scroll and found the place where it was written:

"The Spirit of the Lord is upon me,
    because he has anointed me
      to bring good news to the poor.
He has sent me to proclaim release to the captives
    and recovery of sight to the blind,
      to let the oppressed go free,
to proclaim the year of the Lord's favor."

And he rolled up the scroll, gave it back to the attendant, and sat down. The eyes of all the synagogue were fixed on him. Then he began to say to them, "Today this scripture has been fulfilled in your hearing." (Lk. 4:16–21, NRSV)

Has it indeed been fulfilled? What does that mean? The Greek word translated here as fulfilled, *plerophoreo*, can carry the traditional definitions: to cause a thing to be shown or revealed to the full; or to carry through to the end or accomplish. But it also meant other things: to render inclined or bent on; to make someone certain about something; to persuade or convince someone; to make something fully believed. *Today this scripture has become my intention in your presence. Today this scripture has been fully believed in your hearing. Today I am making you certain about this by your witness.* I interpret that Jesus in his context was establishing his belief and his mission, convincing his people of his inclinations, and revealing his principles fully in a way that made his followers certain of what needed to be done. He asked them to take the risk to fully believe in what he was saying and planning to do.

The announcement in the synagogue was not as much the revelation of a new concept as an intense call to action. Jesus does not have to tell his original audience what he is referring to; they are living the oppression. They exist in the midst of political intrigue, violent uprisings, and constant debate over their fate. They know exactly what he means. And it is a dangerous proposal he is putting out there. His call to arms gets a very mixed reception because he is declaring an all-out, if relatively peacefully waged, war against the construct of the authorities.

What is our responsibility as women of faith to continue fulfilling Jesus' gospel today? The good news included his mission to restore sight to the blind, per the scripture of the prophet Isaiah. Clear-sightedness and a sense of vision were crucial for what he wanted to accomplish. How could anyone enter a new realm or way of being if they could not see it, if they were not convinced it could come pass or intent upon living in it ?

Many people in Jesus' time were blind to what was happening in the world of the Jewish Diaspora under Roman rule. They were resigned to the fact that they had no power over their lives; people were going to suffer (especially the least of these), and there was nothing they could do about it. Among those who were acutely aware of the political climate, many turned a blind eye to the atrocities of the ruling authorities toward the people on the lowest rungs, so that they might feel safe in whatever place they could make for themselves. As long as they could survive, as long as their families were getting by, they did not care what happened to anyone else.

For instance, tax collectors were considered enemies in the Roman-occupied communities because they worked for Roman authorities and took unfair amounts of money from the occupied Jews, even taking their property if they did not have enough money to pay Caesar. These tax collectors would do this to family, friends, and neighbors in order to secure their own places. In Luke 12, Jesus gets frustrated with society's blindness to suffering and how the communal fabric of Jewish society has degraded under the pressure of Roman rule:

> "When you see a cloud rising in the west, you immediately say, 'It is going to rain'; and so it happens. And when you see the south wind blowing, you say, 'There will be scorching heat'; and it happens. You hypocrites! You know how to interpret the appearance of earth and sky; but why do you not know how to interpret the present time? And why do you not judge for yourselves what is right?" (vv. 54–57, NRSV)

Jesus' kind of seeing means looking at the way the world works and using common sense and heart sense to learn what is correct and determine a loving course of action. Once someone helps you see something—gives you new insight—you cannot pretend you do not see it anymore. Refusing to acknowledge and act once you have been shown what is true or right in any given situation forfeits your potential, not to mention the potential of others. It costs lives. It halts the coming of a new and better reality. This is what I believe Jesus meant when he talked about being sinful. Being faithful, then, is taking care to read all the signs around you; creating a new vision aligned with freedom, equality and wholeness; and being committed to acting upon and bringing into reality the future you so clearly see.

This is tremendously difficult. Trust is crucial. Not long ago, I realized I had indeed raised that half-kid the cabbie on Houston Street talked about on Thanksgiving night so many years ago. Coming into my unique wisdom and true purpose was worth the work, worth the wait, worth the pain. And there is always more for us to conceive. It is not easy, but we should not ignore what wants to come forth from us. We are midwives for one other.

A Love Beyond

Outside in the night air, a security guard keeps watch for authorities. Inside, a beautiful young woman named Anis fidgets with her scarf, making sure her hair is completely covered. The band Mavara, for which she plays keyboard, takes the stage to warm up. But at the first sign of trouble they are ready with a plan to shut everything down. They are nervous, not just because they are about to perform, but because they don't know what will happen to them if they are discovered.

The audience begins to arrive. They are also a bit on edge, but motivated by the chance to gather with their underground community to indulge in the music they love. They have heard about the concert through a complex, secret network of texts from unknown cell numbers and word of mouth. They learned the date and time a few days ago, but could not know the location until the last minute, so the cover would not get blown. Because they are citizens of Iran, they could all be arrested and jailed in their own country. The band could have their equipment confiscated, get heavily fined, go to prison, maybe worse.

The progressive rock style of Mavara is unacceptable to the governing religious authorities. Iranian musicians can approach the Ministry of Guidance and Islamic Culture to ask permission to play their music, but if it is not the classical, traditional Persian or sanctioned versions of pop music (which often feature religious lyrics), their music might as well be illegal. Mavara was denied permission because of their genre. If a musician is female, there exists a whole other level of offense. Even if a woman plays or sings music pre-approved by the Ministry, she can only perform to a private audience of women, with no cameras recording and no men on the crew.

An unauthorized woman found playing progressive rock music on stage in front of a mixed crowd could be imprisoned, tortured, or endure any combination and duration of punishments. Anis Oveisi is the only woman in the Iranian progressive rock group Mavara. Despite having her bandmates around her, she stands alone. On this night, as the crowd gathers in a private music school under the auspices of a class, the future is at stake. Think about your greatest desire, your most cherished dream. Then ask yourself if you would truly put your life on the line for it. Most Americans cannot fathom having to make such a choice. But for Anis, making music has always been worth this risk. "I have such a strong desire to make people happy, to create a good time for them" through music, she says.[2]

"I play music and music plays my life," is her mantra. A life without music would not be a life at all. And so she carefully tucks her hair under her hijab, in case authorities raid their performance, since being uncovered on top of playing music illegally would make the punishment more severe. Her keyboard is positioned to the back and side of the stage, for a quicker escape. If they are caught, she is automatically the one in the most trouble.

Anis' Muslim family is supportive, but knowing the risks a woman musician takes, they did once try to influence her so she would not get hurt. They urged her to work for the family business, a popular path for young women, for the basic reason of safety. Women do not often get safe opportunities to work outside the family without running the risk of being sexually harassed, being taken advantage of, or sometimes becoming a sex slave for their employer. Jobs for women are often menial with a very low salary, making it impossible for women to support themselves. Although in the capital city of Tehran the prospects and conditions for professionally trained women have improved, safety is always a big concern. But Anis has never been interested in safety.

She and the band have been in the United States now for less than a year on a music work visa. They still tend to set up in their quick exit formation, Anis poised to the side. But she is emerging in many ways; wearing her hair however she wants, expressing herself more openly, learning to interact with audiences, feeling out her freedoms. Their song "Season of Salvation" haunts listeners with an almost religious tale of a time when spring was the only season, alive and pure, before the human practice of power-over ruined it. But the lyrics bypass all the damnation and pick up on the lessons we learn, the way human beings can look back on past history and create a better future. It is not an unpredictable, exasperated God who rescues condemned sinners, but humans who learn from our mistakes and push on with hope and cooperation toward salvation, with God's unwavering love as guide.

After hearing of Anis' harrowing and triumphant journey from Iran to a new life, I cannot help but wonder how she would advise her younger self. If she could say one thing to young Iranian girls, it would be "don't let go." If you find something you really love doing, she says, then go for it; take advantage of every opportunity no matter the risk. When I ask what she might say to young American girls, she pauses for a moment.

"All that you may complain about—school, clothes, friends—you can still go wherever you want." In light of her overwhelmingly difficult and often terrifying experiences—taking the ultimate risk of leaving home, family, friends, and financial security behind to pursue her dream of making music—she wishes for American women a sense of gravity. "Don't waste your freedom," she says.[3]

I tell Anis' story not to highlight one country's repression of women. I tell it because she reminds us what women have done and how far we have come in our audacity to achieve the impossible—and how far our global society has yet to go. All of the patriarchal Abrahamic religions— Christianity, Islam, Judaism—still have the power to make or break the futures of women and girls. Former President Jimmy Carter has traveled the globe and has a panoramic perspective that few others are able to attain. His latest book, *A Call to Action: Women, Religion, Violence, and Power* recounts stories from his travels and his view of women's lives as an accomplished human rights advocate. The publisher calls it "an impassioned account of the human rights abuses against women and girls around the world, particularly in religious societies."[4] Carter condemns the religiously sanctioned oppression of women and girls he has witnessed:

> This [religious-based] discrimination, unjustifiably attributed to a Higher Authority, has provided a reason or excuse for the deprivation of women's equal rights across the world for centuries. The male interpretations of religious texts and the way they interact with, and reinforce, traditional practices justify some of the most pervasive, persistent, flagrant and damaging examples of human rights abuses.
>
> At their most repugnant, the belief that women must be subjugated to the wishes of men excuses slavery, violence, forced prostitution, genital mutilation and national laws that omit rape as a crime. But it also costs many millions of girls and women control over their own bodies and lives, and continues to deny them fair access to education, health, employment and influence within their own communities.[5]

Patriarchal religion is not just a first-world buzz kill, which is why it is so important for women who have more freedoms and opportunities to raise our voices and reclaim our religious traditions to be used for good instead of evil. We can use everything we have discussed here to forge our own personal spiritual paths. But as Carter Heyward says, "We must realize, actively, that we are meant by God, in whose image we are created, to come into our own, *and to help others do the same*" [emphasis mine].[6] For women of faith, this is the point of our being and believing. It is the point of our freedom.

Theologians Judith Plaskow and Carole Christ put it this way: Activity is the mode of love. Divine revelation, they say in *Weaving the Visions: New*

Patterns in Feminist Spirituality, comes when a community struggles to lay hold of the gift of life, and together weed out all that threatens to snuff out life.[7] Divine revelation comes to us collectively, each woman with her part to play, a piece of the puzzle to contribute. Passive sacrifice of our female potential and authority is not a moral virtue. Plaskow and Christ point out that "this very modern invitation to us women to perceive ourselves under the images of effete gentility, passivity and weakness blocks our capacity to develop a realistic sense of women's historical past."[8] We must hold our history and retain our cultural memory, while fighting for justice in the here and now, and keeping our eyes on what is next to overcome. And what is next takes all of us.

Intensely private faith and individual salvation cannot be a woman's theology. There is too much at stake. Our world needs those who can and will publicly and outwardly bring faith to bear on it. Women historically have been agents of change; but now, more than ever, the future depends upon our collective movement and life-sustaining action. Any suggestion to the contrary about the role of our faith and spiritual practice, say Plaskow and Christ, is a lie meant to control us. Being and doing must never be assumed as polarities at odds with one another in our faith practice. For Plaskow and Christ, this is what a feminist moral theology is all about—the celebration of the intrinsic relationship of being and doing.

I am reminded of the false comparison of Martha and Mary. In Luke 10, Jesus is welcomed into the home of a woman named Martha, who had a sister named Mary. Martha, being the hostess, is doing the work of making the space comfortable, getting people what they need, keeping people fed. Meanwhile, her sister Mary sits at the feet of Jesus, who is teaching. This was an extremely rare, taboo thing for a woman to be allowed to do. Perhaps there is a little uncertain longing on Martha's behalf that her sister has cast aside the traditional women's role and is pushing the boundaries, being a feminist! If only Martha could so confidently cross that line from "women's work" into the male world of learning, thinking, and participation, too. She was nervous. She was not sure how.

It is all so foreign and disorienting that Martha does not know how to frame her question, so she says to Jesus: "Lord, do you not care that my sister has left me to do all the work by myself? Tell her then to help me." Jesus responds, "Martha, you are worried and distracted by many things. Mary has chosen the better part, which will not be taken away from her." But Jesus is not making a judgment about who is right or wrong, or opining about the choice of busily working vs. spending time with Jesus. Instead, he is doing something much more nuanced and life-changing for Martha,

Mary, and other women. He is saying Martha is needlessly concerned in his presence about social norms and gender roles.

Martha is distracted by things outside of her usual scope of reality: her own new hesitation and questioning of her typical female role, and Mary's bold choice. All the while, Jesus does not give heed to gender boundaries or expectations. Jesus acknowledges that Martha is distracted by sexism—held back by what has been deeply ingrained in her regarding where she can or cannot be, who she can or cannot be, what she can or cannot do. He tells her she can be a follower, a disciple, of his way and help bring his vision into reality. He assures Martha that neither will she be judged for not staying in her "woman's place" if she too makes the better choice, which is being part of the group, learning, growing, speaking, participating in his mission. He offers women the unprecedented choice of doing the culturally shocking, scandalous, and offensive thing. And he shows he knows what a scary, hard choice it is for her, considering society's punishments. This story is not a determination of who is "performing Christianity" better: Mary or Martha; it a blatant recognition and calling out of the suppressed situations women find ourselves in, and a call to summon our faith and courage to radically redefine women's place and our work.

In this spirit, Dorothee Soelle uses Martha's contemplation and Mary's participation to create a unified "orthopraxy." Orthopraxy is a correct action or practice, literally an orthodox praxis. It describes the belief that right action is not just an element of religion, it is the core of our faith. For Soelle, Martha and Mary are together an example of both the reflection and action required for wholeness: "Real contemplation gives rise to just actions: theory and praxis are in an indissoluble connection."[9] Martha had to interrogate the situation, come to understand her new options, and set her mind with intention for the shift she would make before she could act on a new reality. Mary boldly moved to participate in a place where she had not been allowed before. She immediately saw an opportunity and let her convictions set her course. Soelle frames the moral of the story with a question: "How are we to think about the relationship between the work we do in the world around us and what we do within ourselves?"[10] They are dependent upon one another.

You have important work to do within yourself and in the world. Take yourself seriously. Reflect deeply on your life and understand your history. You have help in other women; if you reach out for the Elizabeths, you will find genuine reciprocation. Tell your stories without shame or worry about the false images of perfection women are held to...especially female leaders. Do not let intimidation and harsh reactions stop you. Be your beliefs. Proudly reflect your authentic self in your physical being and actions. Keep your unlived life in view. Keep your diverse sisters around the world forefront in your mind. Taking our rightful place in the world, as women, is crucial. As Hillary Clinton said at the Fourth World Conference on Women in Beijing in 1995:

> As long as discrimination and inequities remain so commonplace everywhere in the world, as long as girls and women are valued less, fed less, fed last, overworked, underpaid, not schooled, subjected to violence in and outside their homes—the potential of the human family to create a peaceful, prosperous world will not be realized.[11]

In other words, sight will not be recovered for the blind, the prisoners will not be freed, the oppressed will not be liberated, the jubilee will not be declared, and we will not all take our rightful places in a new realm of God. All the things Jesus said he came to do when he stood up in that small temple and read from the scroll of Isaiah 61 will not be possible without you and your whole presence, your full faithfulness. The gospel will not be fulfilled without you.

Real Love

There seems to be one idea of God that is universal: God is love. But what does that really mean, and how does it manifest? Christians grow up singing "Jesus Loves Me," but the words are trite. Carter Heyward takes it to the next level when she summarizes Jesus' good news: "Love is justice."[12] You cannot say you love someone unless that love is reflecting actions of justice toward the other. If you love people, you struggle with them rather than against them. If you love people, you advocate for them and what they need in order to have abundant life, even if it is different from what you need, even if it seems to threaten your own sense of comfort. Heyward says:

> Among lovers and friends, as well as in our passion for justice for women...true love is the most revolutionary act. To really love is to topple unjust structures, bringing down the principalities and powers of domination and control at all levels of human social relations. Such loving needs no church blessing, although it is good if it is forthcoming.[13]

I am fortunate to be in a church where this is encouraged and practiced. But where it is not, there is a lot to overcome. We must introduce it in corporations, boardrooms, courts, classrooms, trade groups, governments.

Women must bring it everywhere, from local institutions to international systems. We must love in the highest levels of influence. Hillary Clinton has said: "It is past time for women to take their rightful place, side by side with men, in the rooms where the fates of peoples, where their children's and grandchildren's fates, are decided."[14]

Visionaries see injustice in the world and the potential to change it, and they love people by helping others to see what they see. Then they set about dismantling unloving structures, removing the barriers to love, or creating and building new structures to support love. For those who find this idealistic and ethereal, it must be said that real love is gritty, tough, and uncompromising. Love is actually not a feeling, Heyward reminds us. It is a skill and it is difficult; it requires making things right, whether between two people, or among religions, countries, and cultures. Love is a very intense decision and intentional action. Love is an ongoing, never-ending series of difficult choices, and the will to act upon them for the sake of the common good. We express love by promoting and aiding justice. Even if we perceive others as wrong or enemies, we act in love, just as God asks us to—not because it is a religious thing to do, but because it actually works. It changes things. It brings a new reality into being.

Real redeeming love does not say, "Love the sinner, hate the sin." There is simply no place in this whole enterprise to waste time pointing at others and saying we see "sinners" because of their differences or attempts to navigate this world, even if we try make it sound less hypocritical by saying we are sinners ourselves. Sin is our own denial of God's love and avoidance of our unified state with that love. It is the product of destructive doctrine and oppression perpetrated in God's name, which renders us unable to receive God's love for ourselves and therefore recreate and regenerate God's love for others. Sin is to reject an intention or opportunity to love.

Heyward says that the biggest sin women commit is not taking ourselves seriously—not believing that we really matter, or that we can make a difference. Sin is denying that our role in the world, our greatest work, is to be the lover, helping people see. That includes loving ourselves. Love means we will stand up for ourselves, and also unconditionally act on behalf of others. Like Jesus turning over the merchants' tables in the temple, love means we fight for one another, we work for freedom and equality for one another. Heyward says that rage and compassion are equal partners; both are required to create justice.[15]

One of my favorite quotes is from a writer and artist named Brian Andreas. It is part of a series of artwork called "StoryPeople," in which a collective of artists and activists do their thing to help others "experience the world we live in as a world of imagination and possibility and healing."[16] Their website says they create using the valuable power of stories to connect us, but also to protect us: "Isn't it amazing how life sneaks up and steals your memory of who you want to be?" Something about Andreas' quote—on a vividly colored painting that depicts a woman kneeling close to the earth, her hand extended as she beholds a flower rising up to the sun—sums up the gospel to me: *She said she usually cried at least once each day, not because she was sad, but because the world was so beautiful and life was so short.*

If we really live the true gospel, we are going to tear up a little every day, especially when we get frustrated or see injustice—not because we are succumbing to fear, intimidation or lack of hope, but because we so clearly see the unspeakable beauty and potential in ourselves, in one another and in our world, and we know we have something to live for. Because we have eyes to see a new reality, and we know the realm of God is at hand. Because we have something to help save and meaningful work to do. This is how feminists of faith will, in the way of Jesus, bring about the jubilee: a new day of freedom, equality, and justice. This is love. This is the good news.

DEVOTIONAL: **There Is Another Way**

It is love alone that gives worth to all things.—ST. TERESA OF AVILA

I can see God's love only when I become part of it myself.

—DOROTHEE SOELLE

The gospel has been destroyed by religion. It has been twisted to mean that a jealous God required and ordained a violent death to save the souls of an innately depraved humanity from a fiery hell that we deserved. That is not the good news Jesus declared. He modeled calling things as we see them, imagining a new way and believing that world into being. This is what our faith is actually meant to be based upon. From this place, everything changes.

In Genesis 16, Hagar was a young slave girl who belonged to Sarah, Abraham's wife, and lived among Abraham's servants and property. Sarah could not bear children, a threat to her security and worth, so she made Hagar have sex with her husband, forcing her into surrogate motherhood. The story goes that once Hagar became pregnant, Sarah treated her so cruelly, and Abraham was so ambivalent to the abuse, that Hagar ran away into the desert. A place of certain death seemed a respite compared to the uncertainty she endured as a female in her society. God finds and speaks to her in the desert: "Return to your mistress, and submit to her" (v. 9b,

NRSV). This is not literal advice to go back to an abuser, or proof for slavery. (Genesis is a patchwork of redacted traditions reflecting religious and political tales of the day.) We can find a greater mythical takeaway, a way to let Hagar pass the baton to us.

When God finds Hagar, she is by an improbable spring of water in the wilderness. God speaks directly to her, and says her suppression and affliction at the hands of patriarchal society has been recognized. God promises her a future: she will have numerous descendants, which meant social security. He assures her she can go back to her life with a renewed confidence and faith in her redemption. Then the young, beleaguered slave girl becomes the only biblical character to actually name God. "You are *El-roi*," she says to the presence: *the God who sees me*. Likewise, we can trust that who we are and our purpose in the world is not up to the forces who ogle us, define us, intimidate and consume us, but the vision of a God who truly sees us, loves us as we are, and empowers us for change.

When we experience being seen this way, it becomes impossible to retract from the world, even a society that belittles, demeans, and diminishes us. We cannot remove ourselves and ignore it. We are compelled by our faith to go back in and speak up, do our best, ask for help, and love the world into justice. It does no one—including ourselves—any good if we run away, hide our eyes, and cower outside alone. This world is ours too, so we must come back in from the desert and reclaim it. God seeks us out in the desert when we retreat, in the moments we feel we cannot take it anymore. God sees us into being, gives us new vision, and sends us back to help others be seen.

Mary Magdalene is the sole witness to the resurrected Jesus in John 20. He waits for her specifically, waits until she is alone, then calls her by name: "Mary!" Standing in the silent stillness before sunrise, she is the recipient of the original Easter proclamation, the first person to see the revealed Christ: the wisdom and power of God. He wants her to see and accept the new reality, to let it change everything for her, to take it with her and tell the others. Like Mary, in her grief and solitude at the gaping hole of the empty tomb, God calls each of us by name. *There is another way. There is another reality waiting just beyond what you see today.* Femmevangelicals, repent and believe.

NOTES

CHAPTER 1: Finding Your Femmevangelical

[1]Pew Research Religion & Public Life Project, "Nones on the Rise," accessed December 12, 2013, http://www.pewforum.org/2012.10/09/nones-on-the-rise.

[2]Barna Group, "Three Spiritual Journeys of Millennials," accessed December 12, 2013, https://www.barna.org/barna-update/teens-nextgen/612-three-spiritual-journeys-of-millennials#.UyXmx8u9KSM.

[3]Barna Group, State of the Church Series, 2011, "Gender Differences," https://www.barna.org/barna-update/faith-spirituality/508-20-years-of-surveys-show-key-differences-in-the-faith-of-americas-men-and-women#.UyXn6cu9KSM.

[4]Rosemary Radford Ruether, *Sexism and God-Talk: Toward a Feminist Theology* (Boston: Beacon Press, 1993), 16.

[5]Carlene Bauer, *Not That Kind of Girl* (New York: HarperCollins, 2009).

[6]Carlene Bauer, "Someone to Watch Over Me," *Elle* (March, 2013): 402.

[7]Ibid.

[8]From dictionary.com.

[9]See http://www.theatlantic.com/national/archive/2013/11/christian-speaker-tells-public-school-students-how-to-be-dateable/281488/.

[10]Kim Krizan, *Original Sins: Trade Secrets of the Femme Fatale* (Total Global Domination of the Whole World, 2013), back cover.

[11]Check out Donna Freitas' work at donnafreitas.blogspot.com.

[12]Hal Taussig, ed., *A New New Testament: A Bible for the 21st Century Combining Traditional and Newly Discovered Texts* (New York: Houghton Mifflin Harcourt Company, 2013), 179.

CHAPTER 2: A Modern Muse

[1]Eva Shang, personal correspondence with author, fall, 2013.

[2]Ibid.

[3]Steven Hill, "Why Does the US Still Have So Few Women in Office?" *The Nation*, March 7, 2014, http://m.thenation.com/article/178736-why-does-us-still-have-so-few-women-office.

[4]"'I was just 27 and I was butchered': Symphysiotomy victims in their own words," The-Journal.ie, November 6, 2014, accessed November 20, 2014, http://www.thejournal.ie/symphysiotomy-uncat-1356352-Nov2014/

[5]Pope Francis, as quoted in Madeleine Teahan, "I won't create female cardinals, says Pope Francis," *Catholic Herald*, December 16, 2013, accessed February 12, 2014, http://www.catholicherald.co.uk/news/2013/12/16/i-wont-create-female-cardinals-says-pope-francis/.

[6]Jonathan Berr, "The Vatican Bank is busy repenting," *MSN Money*, July 2, 2013, accessed January 3, 2014, http://money.msn.com/now/post—the-vatican-bank-is-busy-repenting.

[7]Georgetown University CARA Catholic Research, accessed February 28, 2014, http://cara.georgetown.edu/caraservices/requestedchurchstats.html.

[8]Tony Jones, "A Challenge to Progressive Theo-Bloggers" on Theoblogy, August 7, 2012, Patheos, http://www.patheos.com/blogs/tonyjones/2012/08/07/a-challenge-to-progressive-theo-bloggers/.

[9]Ibid.

[10]Raymond Tallis, "Not all in the Brain," *Oxford Journals, Brain: A Journal of Neurology* 130 (2007): 11, http://brain.oxfordjournals.org/content/130/11/3050.full

[11]Ibid.

[12]Sheryl Sandberg, *Lean In: Women, Work, and the Will to Lead* (New York: Knopf, 2013).

[13]From http://www.safehorizon.org/page/domestic-violence-statistics—facts-52.html

[14]Reza Aslan, *Zealot: The Life and Times of Jesus of Nazareth* (New York: Random House, 2013).

[15]From https://www.youtube.com/watch?v=RG6uuFWoNdE

[16]My recorded conversation with Reza Aslan.

[17]Ibid.

[18]From www.wellesley.edu/events/commencement/archives/1996commencement.

[19]Hazrat Inayat Khan, "The Struggle of Life (1)," *The Spiritual Message of Hazrat Inayat Khan*, Volume 6, The Alchemy of Happiness.

CHAPTER 3: "In the Beginning" Gets a New Ending

[1]Sue Monk Kidd, *Dance of the Dissident Daughter* (New York: HarperOne, 1996), 2.

[2]Ibid., 1.

[3]Ibid, 228.

[4]Quoted in John Dominic Crossan, *The Power of Parable: How Fiction by Jesus Became Fiction about Jesus* (New York: HarperOne, 2012), 2.

[5]Ibid.

[6]John Dominic Crossan, Introduction to *A New New Testament: A Bible for the 21st Century Combining Traditional and Newly Discovered Texts*, ed. Hal Taussig (New York: Houghton Mifflin Harcourt Company, 2013), xi.

[7]Ibid., xii–xiii.

[8]Ibid., xiv.

[9]Crossan, Introduction to *A New New Testament*, xiii.

[10]Ibid.

[11]Rebecca Traister, "The Single Girl Revolution," *Marie Claire* (May 30, 2012), accessed September 13, 2013, http://www.marieclaire.com/sex-love/single-girl-trend. All quotes attributed to Traister that follow are from this article as well.

[12]For more imformation about this movie, go to http://www.imdb.com/title/tt1800241/?ref_=fn_al_tt_1

[13]Traister, "Single Girl."

[14]See http://www.washingtonpost.com/sports/redskins/nfl-players-wives-seek-role-in-shaping-leagues-domestic-violence-policy/2014/09/27/dd73a608-45ac-11e4-8042-aaf-f1640082e-story.html

[15]Taussig, *A New New Testament*, 226.

[16]Ibid., 217.

[17]Ibid., 219.

[18]Ibid., 224–26.

[19]D.A. Carson, R.T. Francie, J.A. Motyer, and G.J. Wenham, eds., *The New Bible Commentary* (Downers Grove, Ill.: InterVarsity Press, 1994).

[20]Taussig, *A New New Testament*, 500.

[21]Ibid., 501.

[22]Ibid.

[23]Galen Guengerich, *God Revised: How Religion Must Evolve in a Scientific Age* (New York: Palgrave MacMillan, 2013), 9.

[24]Ibid.

[25]Ibid., 37–38.

[26]Ibid., 39–40.

[27]Elaine Pagels, *Adam, Eve, and the Serpent* (New York: Vintage Books, 1988), xxvii–xxviii.

[28]Karen Armstrong, *The Battle for God* (New York: The Ballentine Publishing Group, 2000), xv.

[29]Ibid., xvi.

[30]Ibid., xvii.

[31]Guengerich, *God Revised*, 119.

[32]See http://www.patheos.com/blogs/femmevangelical/2012/07/would-the-biblical-god-laugh-at-toshs-rape-jokes/

[33]Charles R. Swindoll, *Esther: A Woman of Strength and Dignity.* (Nashville: Thomas Nelson, 1997).

[34]Ibid.

[35]Ibid., 36.

[36]Ibid., 37–38.

[37]Ralph Waldo Emerson, "Nature I," in *Nature and Selected Essays* (New York: Penguin Books, 2003), 35.

[38]Delores Williams, *Sisters in the Wilderness* (1993; Maryknoll, NY: Orbis, 2013), 148.

[39]Nora Okja Keller, *Comfort Woman* (Lanham, Md.: Rowman Littlefield, 1999).

[40]Elsa Tamez, ed., *Through Her Eyes: Women's Theology from Latin America* (Eugene, Oreg.: Orbis Book, 1989), v.

[41]Delores Williams, Foreword, in ibid., vi.

[42]Emerson, *Nature.*

[43]Katheryn Pfisterer Darr, "Ezekiel," in *Women's Bible Commentary, Expanded Edition*, ed. Carol A. Newsom and Sharon H. Ringe (Louisville: Westminster John Knox Press, 1998), 192.

CHAPTER 4: Truth and Other Lies

[1]Definition of "dogma," dictionary.com.

[2]Ibid.

[3]From www.ccel.org/ccel/schaff/creeds1.iv.iii.html

[4]Christopher Morse, *Not Every Spirit: A Dogmatics of Christian Disbelief* (Harrisburg, Pa.: Trinity Press International, 1994), 13.

[5]Leo Tolstoy, *Confession* (1885; reprint, New York: W.W. Norton, 1983), 88–91.

[6]Lily Rothman, "A Cultural History of Mansplaining," *The Atlantic*, November 1, 2012, accessed January 17, 2014, http://www.theatlantic.com/sexes/archive/2012/11/a-cultural-history-of-mansplaining/264380/.

[7]John Adams, quoted in ibid.

[8]Ibid.

[9]Tertullian, *De Cultu Feminarum* 1, 12.

[10]Catalyst.org, "Catalyst 2013 Census of Fortune 500: Still No Progress After Years of No Progress," accessed February 21, 2014, http://www.catalyst.org/media/catalyst-2013-census-fortune-500-still-no-progress-after-years-no-progress.

[11]Elaine Pagels, *Adam, Eve, and the Serpent* (New York: Vintage Books, 1988), 84.

[12]Ibid., 85.

[13]Quoted in ibid., xxii.

[14]Ibid., xxiii.

[15]Ibid., xix.

[16]Ibid., 71.

[17]Augustine, *Confessions,* trans. Henry Chadwick (Oxford: Oxford University Press, 1991), II.2, 24.

[18]Ibid., 24.

[19]Pagels, *Adam, Eve, and the Serpent*, xxvi.

[20]Ibid.

[21]Lillie Devereux Blake, *Woman's Place To-day: Four lectures, in reply to the Lenten lectures on "Woman" by the Rev. Morgan Dix* (New York: J.W. Lovell, 1883).

[22]Jeremy Rifkin, *The Empathic Civilization,* accessed February 1, 2014, empathiccivilization.com.

[23]*Miss Representation*, accessed December 15, 2013, film.missrepresentation.org/synopsis.

[24]Sue Monk Kidd, *The Dance of the Dissident Daughter: A Woman's Journey from Christian Tradition to the Sacred Feminine* (New York: HarperCollins, 1996), 72.

[25]From http://www.guttmacher.org/pubs/fb_induced_abortion.html

[26]From http://www.washingtonpost.com/local/maternal-deaths-in-childbirth-rise-in-the-us/2014/05/02/abf7df96-d229-11e3-9e25-188ebe1fa93b_story.html

[27]See http://www.whitehouse.gov/blog/2014/01/24/weekly-address-taking-action-end-sexual-assault.

[28]See Rape, Abuse Incest National Network, http://www.rainn.org/get-information/statistics/sexual-assault-offenders.

[29]See Rape, Abuse Incest National Network, http://www.rainn.org/statistics.

[30]Catalyst.org, "Catalyst's New Report Reveals Key Trends Impacting Women in the World," accessed February 21, 2014, http://www.catalyst.org/media/catalysts-new-report-reveals-key-trends-impacting-women-world.

[31]The New Evangelical Partnership for the Common Good, "A Call to Common Ground on Family Planning," accessed November 14, 2014, https://www.youtube.com/watch?v=0pmIXEqQV88list=PL3K3pWilzqCxB_kF1otNlxLjO-77aPdf8.

[32]From depravedwretch.com website.

[33]See http://www.nydailynews.com/news/national/fla-deadly-theater-shooting-texting-son-article-1.1720738

[34]See http://www.cnn.com/2014/09/09/opinion/costello-blaming-janay-rice-outrageous/

[35]Pagels, *Adam, Eve, and the Serpent*, 71.

[36]The Gnostic Society Library, The Nag Hammadi Library, "The Gospel of Philip," trans. Wesley W. Isenberg, http://gnosis.org/naghamm/gop.html. Accessed August 27, 2014.

[37]Ibid.

[38]Ibid.

[39]Paul Tillich, *The Courage to Be* (New Haven and London: Yale University Press, 2000), 190.

[40]Brian McLaren, "The Church in America Today," in *A New Evangelical Manifesto: A Kingdom Vision for the Common Good*, ed. David P. Gushee (St. Louis: Chalice Press, 2012), 3.

[41]Morse, *Not Every Spirit*, 5.

[42]Pagels, *Adam, Eve, and the Serpent*, 66.

[43]*Reality of the Rulers*, trans. Bentley Layton, accessed February 28, 2014, http://gnosis.org/naghamm/hypostas.html.

CHAPTER 5: Pinnacle of Womanhood

[1]Shaye J.D. Cohen, "Legitimization Under Constantine," *Frontline*, accessed December 11, 2013, http://www.pbs.org/wgbh/pages/frontline/shows/religion/why/legitimization.html.

[2]Ibid.

[3]Ibid.

[4]Ibid.

[5]Ibid.

[6]Gloria Feldt, *No Excuses: Nine Ways Women Can Change How We Think about Power* (Berkeley, Calif.: Seal Press, 2012), 66.

[7]Ibid., 81.

[8]Feldt, *No Excuses*.

[9]Ibid.

[10]Laurie Goodstein, "Vatican Reprimands a Group of U.S. Nuns and Plans Changes," *The New York Times*, April 18, 2012, accessed January 28, 2014.

[11]Ibid.

[12]Ibid.

[13]See Guttmacher Institute, "Religion and Contraception Use," http://www.guttmacher.org/media/resources/Religion-FP-tables.html

[14]Judy Roberts, "Nuns on the Bus 2," *National Catholic Register*, June 6, 2013, accessed January 1, 2014, http://www.ncregister.com/daily-news/nuns-on-the-bus-2/.

[15]Sojourner Truth, "Ain't I a Woman?" *Modern History Sourcebook*, Fordham University, accessed February 20, 2014, http://www.fordham.edu/halsall/mod/sojtruth-woman.asp.

[16]Ibid.

[17]Ibid.

[18]Ibid.

[19]Ann Marie Slaughter, "Yes, You Can: Sheryl Sandberg's 'Lean In'," *The New York Times*, March 7, 2013, accessed February 2, 2014, http://www.nytimes.com/2013/03/10/books/review/sheryl-sandbergs-lean-in.html?pagewanted=all_r=0.

[20]Sheryl Sandberg, *Lean In: Women, Work, and the Will to Lead* (New York: Random House, 2013).

[21]Personal interview, fall 2013.

[22]See http://themysteryofchrist.wordpress.com/2012/09/21/joan-chittister-the-inner-journey.

[23]Silvia Schroer, "The Book of Sophia," in *Searching the Scriptures, Volume Two: A Feminist Commentary*, ed. Elisabeth Schüssler Fiorenza (New York: The Crossroad Publishing Company, 1994), 25.

[24]Ibid., 17.

[25]Ibid., 29–30.

[26]Ibid., 33.

[27]Ibid., 29.

[28]Kidd, *Dance of the Dissident Daughter*, 149.

CHAPTER 6: Being is Believing

[1]HeForShe.org.

[2]Eric Fromm, *The Anatomy of Human Destructiveness* (New York: Henry Holt and Company, Inc., 1973), 438.

[3]Elisabeth Schüssler Fiorenza, *In Memory of Her: A Feminist Theological Reconstruction of Christian Origins* (New York: The Crossroads Publishing Company,1983), 153.

[4]Eric Fromm, *Escape from Freedom* (1941; rep. New York: H. Holt, 1994).

[5]Max Weber (and other sociologists and philosophers) famously noted the almost manic "Protestant work ethic" that developed once the heavy hand of the Catholic Church's controlling rule was lifted after the Reformation. This eventually lead to a competitive capitalism (and capitalism or market force as religion) that did not rest and always wanted more, even after basic needs were met. For more on this, see *The Protestant Ethic and the Spirit of Capitalism*, ed. Peter Baehr and Gordon Wells (New York: Penguin Books, 2002).

[6]Fromm, *Escape from Freedom*.

[7]Sue Monk Kidd, *The Dance of the Dissident Daughter: A Woman's Journey from Christian Tradition to the Sacred Feminine* (New York: HarperCollins, 1996).

[8]Ibid.

[9]Adam Phillips, *Missing Out: In Praise of the Unlived Life* (New York: Farrar, Straus and Giroux), xix.

[10]Ibid.

[11]Andrea Gibson, "Thank Goodness," in *The Madness Vase* (Long Beach, Calif.: Write Bloody Publishing, 2012).

[12]Dorothee Soelle, *The Silent Cry: Mysticism and Resistance* (Minneapolis: Fortress Press, 2001), 13.

[13]Ibid,13.

[14]Ibid., 14.

[15]See Summer's Eve commercial, accessed March, 2014, http://m.youtube.com/watch?v=1k8iaCjSiBQ.

[16]Soelle, *The Silent Cry*, 285.

[17]Definition from "embody," dictionary.com.

[18]See http://www.alternet.org/gender/deeply-disturbing-truth-about-street-harassment-america, http://youtu.be/b1XGPvbWn0A and http://www.alternet.org/gender/if-you-were-shocked-viral-street-harassment-video-youre-probably-man

[19]See https://www.youtube.com/watch?v=fMjavRu4v5c.

[20]See http://www.newsweek.com/why-no-one-talking-about-second-steubenville-rape-case-207333.

[21]See http://www.polarisproject.org, one of several initiatives to address the problem of human trafficking.

[22]Kidd, *Dissident Daughter*, 218.

[23]Renita Weems, *Showing Mary: How Women Can Share Prayers, Wisdom, and the Blessings of God* (New York: Warner Books, 2002).

[24]Ibid., 26.

[25]Ibid., 27–28.

[26]Andrew Newberg, Eugene D'Aquili, and Vince Rause, *Why God Won't Go Away: Brain Science and the Biology of Belief (*New York: Ballantine Books, 2001).

[27]Ibid., 8.

[28]Ibid., 109.

[29]Joel Khan, "7 Scientific Reasons You Should Listen to Your Heart (Not Your Brain)," *Mind, Body, Green,* December 16, 2013, accessed January 3, 2014, http://www.mindbodygreen.com/0-11982/7-scientific-reasons-you-should-listen-to-your-heart-not-your-brain.html.

[30]Ibid.

[31]Ibid.

[32]Christine Valters Paintner, *Lectio Divina—The Sacred Art: Transforming Words Images into Heart-Centered Prayer* (Woodstock, Vt.: Skylight Paths Publishing, 2011), xi–xii.

[33]Ibid., 9.

[34]Ibid., xii.

[35]Audre Lorde and Cheryl Clarke, *Sister Outsider: Essays and Speeches by Audre Lorde* (New York: Crown Publishing Group, 2007), 36.

[36]Robert M. Grant, trans., "The Gospel of Truth," The Gnostic Society Library, The Nag Hammadi Library, http://gnosis.org/naghamm/got.html

[37]Rumi, Mevlana Jalaluddin, *The Pocket Rumi, ed. Kabir Helminski* (Boston: Shambhala Publications, Inc., 2001), 138.

CHAPTER 7: She's Got the Whole World in Her Hands

[1]From "clairvoyant," dictionary.com.

[2]Conversation with Anis Oveisi in November, 2013.

[3]Ibid.

[4]Julie Bosman, "Jimmy Carter Book on Women's Rights Is Set for March Release," *The New York Times,* January 28, 2014, http://www.nytimes.com/2014/01/29/business/media/jimmy-carter-book-on-womens-rights-is-set-for-march-release.html?_r=0.

[5]Jimmy Carter, "The words of God do not justify cruelty to women," *The Guardian/The Observer,* July 11, 2009, accessed November 11, 2014, http://www.theguardian.com/commentisfree/2009/jul/12/jimmy-carter-womens-rights-equality.

[6]Carter Heyward, *Our Passion for Justice: Images of Power, Sexuality, and Liberation* (Cleveland: Pilgrim Press, 1984), 4.

[7]Judith Plascow and Carole Christ, *Weaving the Visions: New Patterns in Feminist Spirituality* (New York: Harper Collins, 1989), 214.

[8]Ibid., 218.

[9]Dorothee Soelle, *The Silent Cry: Mysticism and Resistance* (Minneapolis: Fortress Press, 2001), 201.

[10]Ibid., 199.

[11]See http://www.feminist.com/resources/artspeech/inter/hill.htm.

[12]Heyward, *Our Passion for Justice*, 85.

[13]Ibid., 83.

[14]See http://www.feminist.com/resources/artspeech/inter/hill.htm.

[15]Heyward, *Our Passion for Justice*, 83.

[16]See http://www.storypeople.com.